MISSIONARY EDUCATION IN INDIA

MISSIONARY EDUCATION IN INDIA

HENRY HUIZINGA

GYAN

Published by

Gyan Publishing House
5, Ansari Road
Daryaganj, New Delhi-110002
Phone: 011-47034999, 9811692060
E-mail: books@gyanbooks.com

Distribution Network
gyanbooks.com
India, USA, Canada, UK, Australia

ISBN: 978-93-7133-267-5 (PB)

First Published, 1909

2nd Impression 2025

Printed at: Gyan Press, Delhi.

MISSIONARY EDUCATION IN INDIA
Author Henry Huizinga

Missionary Education in India.

Missionary Education in India

By

REV. HENRY HUIZINGA, M.A., PH.D.,

Vice Principal, and Professor of English,

American Baptist Mission College, Ongole, India.

A Thesis submitted to the Faculty of the Department of Literature. Science and the Arts of the University of Michigan for the degree of Doctor of Philosophy and published by the author in accordance with the requirements of the University.

PREFACE.

The following Thesis is an attempt to set forth the contribution of Protestant Christian Missions to the Education of India. In 1891 Mr. F. W. Thomas, of Cambridge, wrote the Le Bas Prize Essay on British Education in India, in which Missionary Education is mentioned now and then. In 1899 the Rev. William I. Chamberlain wrote a Doctor's Thesis, for Columbia University, on Education in India, following largely along the lines of Mr. Thomas and bringing the subject up to date. But very slight mention is made of Missionary Education. The present Thesis is, in a way, a complement to the fore-going, and tells the story of a distinct portion of Education in India. It is largely historical and as such is a compilation of various sources mentioned in in the Bibliography. The Statistics on pp. 88-94 and 129-135 are the result of very careful study of original sources, and are the latest and most accurate available. These show the amount of Missionary Education and its ratio to the whole education of India. It is for these pages that the Thesis was partly planned, for they show the part that missionaries are contributing to the work of education in India, and the obligation that the people of India and India's Government are under to them for this work. The Second part, or the Theory of Missionary Education, though not entirely new, for its aim is to reflect the views of the main body of missionaries now at work, is a complete statement and a fresh grouping of the distinct aims and the unique results, together with the problems and needs, of Missionary Education in India.

Special acknowledgements are due to the Rev. S. D. Bawden, B. Sc. for valuable assistance in reading proof.

Contents.

INTRODUCTORY.

	Page
Extent of Country	1
Classes of People	1
Civilization and Education	2
Invasions and Conquests of India	3
Political: Aryan, Muhammadan, European.	
Spiritual: Brahmanism, Buddhism, Muhammadanism, Christianity.	
Methods of Missionary Work	4
Preaching, Literary, Healing, Education.	
Education subdivided: Secular and Literary, Training of Workers, Medical, Industrial	5
The First only the Subject of this Thesis	5
Different Systems of Education in India	6
Indigenous, Government, Missionary.	
Relation of these to Each Other	7

PART I.

THE HISTORY OF MISSIONARY EDUCATION IN INDIA.

CHAPTER I.

MISSIONARY EDUCATION BEFORE 1830 ...	8-18
Early Jesuit Attempts. Xavier's College at Goa ...	8
Dutch Reformed Church in Ceylon	8
First Protestant Missions at Tranquebar, 1706	9-10
Their Schools, Difficulties. First Theological School at Cuddalore. John Kiernander's Schools in North India. Swartz's Great Work. Dr. C. S. John.	

William Carey and the Other Serampore Brethren ... 10-12

A New Movement. Connection with Fort William College 10

Carey's Zeal for Translation and Education ... 11

The Serampore College 11

Objects and Methods described by Dr. Marshman 12

The London Missionary Society 12-14

Mr. Forsythe and Mr. May around Calcutta 12

Notice of the Work by the Governor-General and First Grant-in-aid 13

Work in Tinnevelly, Nagercoil, and Madras 13-14

The Society for the Propagation of the Gospel 14

Bishop Middleton's College on the Hooghly.

The Scottish Missionary Society 14

Vigorous Educational Work around Bankot near Bombay.

The Church Missionary Society 14-16

The Raja Jay Narayan presents a School to Mr. Corrie 15

Work in Bombay. Among the Syrian Christians at Cottayam. Tinnevelly: Struggles and Subsequent Marvellous Success 15-16

The American Congregationalists 16

Haystack Meeting. The Dispersion at Calcutta.

School Work in Bombay and in Ceylon.

Independent or Union Societies 17

Calcutta School Book Society.

British and Foreign School Society. First Lady Educational Missionary, Miss Cooke. Patronage of the Machioness of Hastings, An Indian Prince's Munificent Gift.

Bombay School Book Society.

Christian Knowledge Society at Madras.

Summary. Figures and Nature of Work 17-18

CHAPTER II.

MISSIONARY EDUCATION IN INDIA, 1830-1882 19-57

(1) ALEXANDER DUFF, 1830-1878 19-42

Duff's Arrival. His Fitness for the Time 19

The Place of Operations 19

English Government Operations Previous to Duff ... 20
Madrissa, or Muhammadan College at Calcutta 20
Sanskrit College at Benares 20
Hindu College at Calcutta, founded by Rammohun Roy 20
Duff's Tour of Inspection 20-22
Previous Attempts to conquer Brahmanism a Failure 21
Duff's Own Plan Different from Others ... 21-22
Duff's Helpers: Lord Bentinck, Rajah Rammohun Roy 22-24
Rammohun Roy's Early Life and Struggles after Light 23
Meeting with Duff. Helps in getting a Building and Scholars 23-24
Duff's First Teaching 24-27
First Public Examination. Popularity of the School 25
Influence of Religious Teaching 25
English Lectures and First Converts 26-27
The New Charter of 1833 27-31
Controversy between Orientalists and Moderns 27-28
Duff's Part and Influence in deciding the Controversy 28-30
Macaulay's Minute the End of the Controversy 30
Lord Bentinck's Tribute to Duff 31
Duff' Second Term 32-36
Changes since He First came to India ... 32-33
Success of the New Learning 33
Renewal of the Controversy. Duff assails Lord Auckland 34-35
Lord Hardinge's Minute recognizes Christian Schools 35-36
The Halifax Despatch 36-42
Duff's Testimony before the Parliamentary Commission 36-37
His Authorship of the Despatch 38
Summary of the Despatch 38-42
(2) THE GROWTH AND EXTENSION OF MISSIONARY EDUCATION 1830-1882 43-57
John Wilson in Bombay 43-47
Wilson College and Its Converts 44-45
Wilson's Part in Government Legislation ... 45-47
John Anderson in Madras 47-49

Madras Christian College Founded. Early Converts 47
Girls Schools. Conversions of Girls 48
John Murdoch and the Christian Vernacular Education Society, (Later, The Christian Literature Society) 49-50
Other American and English Societies during this period 51-56
Congregationalists, Reformed, Baptists, ... 51
Methodists, Presbyterians, Institution for Girls at Dehra Doon 52
English Baptists, ... 53-54
London Missionary Society, ... 54
Church Missionary Society 54-56
Cathedral Mission College, Noble College 55
St. John's College 55-56
Summary and General Characterization 56-57
Education of Girls and Women 56-57

CHAPTER III.

THE EDUCATION COMMISSION, 1882-1883 ... 58-71
Dissatisfaction with the Educational Department for its Method of carrying out the Despatch of 1854 ... 58-60
Missionary Agitators in India and in England ... 58
Points of Grievance :—
(1) Neglect of Primary Education ... 59
(2) Fostering of Government Colleges 59
(3) The Education of the Masses not keeping Pace with the Growth of the Population 59
(4) Aided Education not encouraged ... 59-60
(5) Unfair Treatment of Mission Schools 60
Appointment of the Commission. Synopsis of Their Report 61-71
Indigenous Education 62
Primary Education 62-63
Secondary Education 63-64
Collegiate Education 64
Moral Teaching and a Moral Text-book recommended by the Commission but disallowed by Government 64
Conscience Clause recommended by the Commission but disallowed by Government ... 65
External Relations to the Department ... 65

Grant-in-aid 66
Question of Sympathy of the Department for Aided Schools 66-67
Withdrawal of the State from Education ... 67-68
Withdrawal not to be in Favor of Mission Schools 68-69
Female Education 69
Statistics and Needs 70-71

CHAPTER IV.

MODERN MISSIONARY EDUCATION, 1882-1907 72-94
Reasons for a New Impulse and Larger Growth ... 72
Dr. William Miller 73-74
Dr. D. Mackichan. Dr. J. C. R. Ewing and Others ... 74
Summary of Missionary Education during this Period ... 75-82
American Societies: Congregationalists 75
Baptists 75-76
Presbyterians 76
Lutherans 76-77
Methodists 77
British Societies: Society for the Propagation of the Gospel and the Church Missionary Society ... 77-79
Wesleyan Missionary Society 79
London Missionary Society 79
Church of Scotland Mission and the United Free Church of Scotland 79-82
Duff College, and the General Assembly's Institution, Calcutta 80
Wilson College, Bombay 80
The Madras Christian College 81
The Universities Commission, 1902 82-88
The Part of Missionaries in Movements for Reform ... 82
Lord Curzon's Administration and Reforms in Education 83-84
Missionary Work not Specifically affected at this Time ... 85
The Question of Second Grade Colleges 85-86
Government of Madras ignoring Aided Education ... 87-88
Strength of Missionary Education: Statistics. 88-94
Growth during the Period, 1882-1907 88
Christian Colleges in India 89
Comparison of Educational and Ecclesiastical Work 89

The Education of Christians ahead of the Remaining Population 90-91
Number of Missionaries engaged in Educational Work 91
Amount of Expenditure on Missionary Education 91-93
Summary of Figures 93-94

PART II.

THE THEORY OF MISSIONARY EDUCATION.

CHAPTER I.

THE AIM OF MISSIONARY EDUCATION ... 95-104
Missionary Education for the Christian Community ... 95-96
Training of Christian Workers 95-96
Education of Christian Children 96
Schools for Non-Christian Children 96
High Schools 96-97
Colleges 97
The Aims of Christian Higher Education for Non-Christians 97-104
The Educational Aim 98-99
The Evangelistic Aim 99-100
Missionary Education a Preparation for the Gospel 100-103
Unity of Aim in Educational Work 103-104

CHAPTER II.

THE RESULTS OF MISSIONARY EDUCATION 105-116
Difficulty of tabulating Results 105
Unique Results among Non-Christians considered ... 105-112
1. It has imparted True Notions of Christianity 106-107
2. It creates Feelings of Friendliness 107-109
3. It has proved the Best Means of winning Converts from the Higher Classes 109
4. It has imparted a New Spirit and New Ideals in Hindu Life Itself 109-111
5. Moral Influence of the Teaching of the Bible 111
6. Influence on Social Progress 112

Testimonies to the Value of Educational Missions ... 112-116
Sir William Muir. Lord Dufferin 113
Resolution of the Bangalore Missionary Conference 113-114
Resolution of the Madras Missionary Conference, 1902 114
Testimony of Dr. Dennis and Dr. Warneck ... 114-115
Testimony of Mr. John R. Mott 116

CHAPTER III.

PROBLEMS AND NEEDS OF MISSIONARY EDUCATION 117-128
1. Christian and Non-Christian Teachers 117-121
Scarcity of Christian Teachers 117
Conversion of Teachers 118
Proportion of Christian and Non-Christian Teachers 119
Need of More Missionary Teachers. Their Training 119-121
2. The Place of Religious Teaching in Mission Schools 121-123
How to interest Students in Religious Teaching 121-122
The Question of Christian School Readers ... 122-123
3. The Harmony of Christian Education with the Aims of the People 123-125
Want of Harmony between the School and the Home 124
Testimony of a Social Leader 124
An Objection from "*The Hindu*" to Compulsory Religious Teaching 125
4. Need of Extension 125-128
Number of Uneducated 126
Need of Education for Christian Children ... 126-127
The Great Need for More and Better Equipped Christian Colleges 127-128
STATISTICAL TABLES 129-135
Abbreviations 129
Protestant Christian Colleges in India, with Statistical Information concerning them 130-132
Roman Catholic Colleges, ditto 133
General and Educational Statistics of Various Societies ... 134-135
Bibliography 136-138
Biographical Note 139
Index 140-141

Missionary Education in India.

INTRODUCTORY.

India is a great and interesting country. It extends from east to west about 2,500 miles and from north to south nearly 2,000 miles, and its area is 1,766,642 square miles, equal to the whole of Europe, excluding Russia, or to half the United States of America. Its population is nearly four times that of the United States, and there in that middle peninsula of southern Asia, live nearly as many people as in North America, South America, and Africa combined.

The inhabitants of India are not a homogeneous people, but differ from each other in race, color, customs, and religion. More than a hundred languages are spoken, some of which are as different from others as English is from Hebrew. Roughly speaking, there are four easily distinguishable kinds of people, who have lived side by side in India for many generations :—1. The Brahmans and Rajputs, forming about ten per cent. of the population. 2. Sudras and mixed Hindus, forming the middle classes, the traders, artisans, farmers, making up about sixty per cent. 3. Muhammadans, partly descendants of Turks and Arabians and partly a mixed race, but everywhere sharply defined and distinguished from the other races, forming about twenty per cent. of the people. 4. The Aborigenes and out-castes, variously called pariahs, sweepers, panchamas, etc., making up the remaining ten per cent. of India's population.

The ancient history of India is not well known, when it comes to questions of dates, but we are in a position to make out much of the civilization and life and thought of old Hindustan from its literature, which is among the oldest in the world, and from the fact that so much of the old life has been preserved in the customs and traditions of the people. Ancient India was not a savage country, for people who produced a literature such as the Sanskrit, with its lyrics and dramas and epics; who maintained schools in every village; who not only taught every Brahman boy to write, but taught systems of deep philosophy, astronomy, mathematics, and medical science; were not savages, though they did not have railroads and other modern inventions.

Education in olden times was almost wholly confined to the Brahman class. All the great works of Sanskrit literature were produced by them, and to them also was due nearly all the progress that was made in the sciences. The Muhammadans shared to some extent in the latter, and independently cultivated the Arabic and Persian languages and literatures. Occasionally one of the middle classes stole the sacred fire of knowledge, and some poets even from among the out-castes achieved distinction, at least one of them a woman. But it remained true that practically all in three of the classes named above, forming nine-tenths of the population, were illiterate. The Brahmans looked after the education of their male children only, for education of any sort was not thought of for girls even among them. A small class of women, who served in temples and were immoral, were taught to read and write, and more important, to sing and dance. Even to-day, after more than seventy-five years of organized educational effort on the part of the British government, there are still less than fifteen million men and boys and less than one million women and girls who can read and write : and there are 277,728,485 people who are wholly ignorant of written or printed characters in any language.

The history of India can be remembered best as a series of invasions and conquests. There were the early Aryan invasions in remote antiquity : then the Muhammadan invasions all through the Middle Ages : and lastly, the European invasions by the Portuguese, Dutch, Danish, French, and English. There have been invasions and conquests of a different sort, usually more or less closely associated with the former, that have dealt more with the intellect and spirit of the people. Such were Brahman sacerdotalism, Buddhistic atheism, Muhammadan fatalism, and lastly, Christianity. The first was introduced by the Aryans as they invaded the territory of the dark races; the second arose from within the land; the third was brought by the Muhammadan invaders as a part of the spirit of their conquest; the last was not part and parcel of the invasion of European traders or conquerors, on the contrary, it was resisted and opposed by them; and for a long time while other religions and their votaries were protected in their rights, the Christian religion and its missionaries were not tolerated by the Christian government of Britain.

But these days are luckily past, and to-day India is of all lands the most open to the gospel. With a powerful government pledged to religious neutrality, affording religious liberty and free speech and press throughout the country, missionaries can pursue their chosen work among all classes of the people without fear of molestation. Not only are their lives and property safe, but special protection is afforded to all the inhabitants of the land to practise whatever old or new religion their consciences direct. Missionaries have taken advantage of such a great opportunity, and there is no land where more systematic efforts have been made and where mission work of all kinds is better organized than in India. With a force of 1,900 men and 2,500 women, in all, 4,400 Protestant foreign missionaries, coming nine-tenths of them from England and America, and the others from continental Europe and Australia, and with an army of over 37,000 Indian workers, they are busily engaged in every nook and corner of the empire endeavoring in various ways to establish the kingdom of Christ. The 657 Roman Catholic missionaries bring the number of foreign missionaries to over 5,000, and these together with all the Indian workers, Catholic and Protestant, make an army of 50,000 working to-day for the spiritual conquest of India.

Many different forms and methods of work have been engaged in by missionaries, but nearly all can be reduced to the following four kinds:—(1) *Preaching*. Missionaries began with the direct proclamation of the gospel. John 3: 16, and Mathew 11 : 28, formed the burden of their message, which concerned itself almost entirely with spiritual affairs belonging to a future life. This part of the work still bulks large in all their efforts. (2) *Literary*. From the very beginning of Protestant missions the translation of the Bible has formed an important part of their work, and with this is to be classed the formation of commentaries, hymn books, and other Christian literature. (3) *Healing*. Medical missions have been found an important handmaid to preaching, especially as a means of opening people's hearts and so preparing the way for the Word of God. (4) *Education*. The work of training the young has always been deemed a legitimate part of mission work.

This may be divided into several branches :—(*a*) A system of organized secular education, combined with religious education, beginning with the primary department up to the Master's and Doctor's degrees in the university. (*b*) Training schools for spiritual workers, such as theological seminaries, and Bible schools for preparing both men and women evangelists and preachers. (*c*) Medical training institutions, mostly for training nurses and doctors' helpers. (*d*) Industrial schools, for teaching trades and commercial branches. These cannot always be entirely separated, for in practice the various forms of training are often joined together, as where literary classes are held in connection with a trade school, or where a secular education is given as a part of an Indian preacher's training. The educational missionary not infrequently preaches the gospel, both in the class room and in the streets, thus doing the work of an evangelist; and almost every preaching missionary has in his field a number of schools which he must supervise.

The following thesis will, however, treat of the first kind only, as far as that can be distinguished from the other branches; and our most serious attention will be devoted to the upper departments of the organized system of education as carried on by Protestant missionary bodies in India. Missionary Education, as thus defined, is open to all classes of the people, and is intended as well for non-Christians as for Christians. The aims may be different though the methods are very much the same. The aims may be wholly unlike in the upper and lower departments of education, or for different classes of the people, still one general purpose runs through it all. That is, that missionaries believe that education under Christian auspices, pervaded by the spirit and aims of a Christian purpose, is a useful and helpful stimulus to social progress, an effective instrument of social regeneration, and as such is counted a noble and legitimate missionary instrumentality.

In considering the subject of education in India we must bear in mind that there are three factors to be reckoned with. There is first, indigenous education, beginning from very ancient times; second, the public system of education, or British education, inaugurated and supported by the British government; and third, Missionary Education, carried on by Christian missionaries. The first of these has been much modified and has been largely merged into the others, while also the remaining two have become so nearly alike in their methods, that there exists to-day only one system of education in India. In fact, as will appear in the sequel, it has been the policy of the British government in India to delegate the whole work of education as much as possible to private bodies and individuals, whoever are willing to undertake the task, while she herself holds a guiding hand and gives such assistance as is required to call forth private effort. Not only missionaries have availed themselves of this policy, but the promoters of other religions or of some special kind of social reform as well, and even many groups of private individuals and municipalities have in this manner by the means of government aid sought to provide for the educational needs of their communities. For the most part these various undertakings are so small as not to warrant any special notice, or else they are so nearly conformed to and identical with the government system of education as not to admit of separate treatment. But Missionary Education, embracing about one-eighth of the whole number of those taught and nearly one-third of the students in colleges, is of sufficient bulk to give considerable color to the whole scheme. It has, moreover, a history of its own and has from the beginning had a marked influence on the government system, which it will be profitable to trace. And while to-day it has become wonderfully harmonized with surrounding efforts, those engaged in the work and those most intimately concerned believe that it still has a distinct purpose to fulfil, that it is neither a rival nor a mere helper of government, but that its object is higher and its sphere is wider. In the following pages, we shall trace in the First Part the History of Missionary Education; we shall follow its growth and try to see the situations as they presented themselves to those engaged in the work. And then, in the Second Part, we shall present the Theory of Missionary Education, in which we shall show the relation that it has to other forms of educational effort in India as well as to other departments of missionary work, and we shall indicate the influence that Missionary Education has had and has on the individual and national life of the people. All this inquiry, it may be said, will be carried on in a spirit of sympathy with the broad objects of Missionary Education; and the worthiness of the general aim of all missionary work in obedience to the command of the Lord Jesus Christ will be taken for granted.

PART I.

THE HISTORY OF MISSIONARY EDUCATION IN INDIA.

CHAPTER I.

MISSIONARY EDUCATION BEFORE 1830.

Many attempts have been made to convert India to Christianity, the earliest of which, beginning soon after the time of the apostles, took place without leaving any distinct records : still, there have been Christians of the Syrian type in India throughout the Christian era, and to-day they number over half a million souls. They never exerted much influence over the surrounding population and have long lived as though they were one of the castes of Hinduism, and their mark on the education of India has been small. Nor does the early Jesuit attempt concern us here, except to note that Xavier in 1542 established the first Jesuit college in the world, the first Christian college in India, at Goa on the west coast, largely for the purpose of training Indian preachers. The Dutch Reformed Church sent its missionaries along with the traders of the Dutch East India Company, and when they succeeded in 1658 in overcoming the Portuguese power in Ceylon, the Reformed Church of Holland was established as the religion of the new colony. Public proclamation informed the inhabitants that baptism, communion in the state church, and subscription to the Helvetic Confession were essential preliminaries not only to appointment to office but even to farming land. Is it any wonder that the "converts" soon numbered half a million, or a fourth of the total population of the island? But little or nothing was done for the instruction of the people in the principles of the Christian religion.

Protestant missions are usually held to begin with the arrival in Tranquebar, South India, of the Danish missionaries, Ziegenbalg and Plutschau, in 1706. Almost from the first these men established religious schools for the instruction of the slaves of the Danish settlement. In six years the number of converts had reached 250 and a boarding school had been established with 78 pupils, most of whom were supported by the missionaries. Soon the favor of the Danish government was secured for the education of the natives, and 21 schools were established, in some of which the missionaries were allowed to place Christian teachers to expound the truths of Christianity. In 1717 Ziegenbalg commenced a school in Cuddalore, Arcot District, and in it the first ordained Indian minister was educated. A part of the work of the early missionaries, besides preaching and translating the Scriptures, was the preparation of school manuals. We can hardly realize the difficulties under which these men labored all through the first century and a half, so few in number, with very little support from the home churches, persecuted not only by non-Christians, but by Christian governments, and often cast into prison. Missionary work was a new venture and paths had to be blazed wherever a new policy was attempted. It is doubtful if education was regarded as a method of evangelism, and the schools that were established were of a most elementary character, intended to instruct catechumens in the creed preparatory to baptism and sometimes to teach the children of converts. In 1758 one of the Danish missionaries, John Kiernander, went to the north of India and besides evangelistic work started a school which soon enrolled 200 pupils. He was one of the most zealous pioneers and was perhaps the first missionary in India to introduce the education of non-Christian children as an evangelistic agency. Christian Friedrich Swartz arrived at Tranquebar in 1750, a man of indefatigable zeal, earnest devotion, and great wisdom. He travelled hundreds of miles, mostly on foot, and visited Madras, Cuddalore, Negapatam, Tanjore, Trichinopoly, Kumbakonum, covering nearly the whole of South India. He was very careful to husband the fruits of his labors by the establishment of schools, appointing teacher catechists over them, which served as nuclei of Christian congregations and fostered the growth of religious principles among them. We also read of Dr. C. S. John, who labored in Tranquebar forty-two years, and who in 1812 shortly before he died established 20 free reading schools which enrolled over 600 pupils. Such were the meager efforts of the first century of Protestant missions on behalf of education in India.

William Carey arrived in India in 1793, and with him a new era of Protestant missions was begun. For the first time Christianity was entirely disconnected from any secular power, and this resulted at first unfavorably to the quantity of the work but wholly favorably to its quality. After seven years the first convert was baptized. The missionaries had to struggle for their own support, for the people at home were not trained to give for the cause. On this account, Mr. and Mrs. Marshman, co-laborers with Carey, opened two boarding schools for children of English traders, but in 1800 Carey was appointed to the chair of Sanskrit and Bengali in the new Government college at Fort William on a salary of $7,500, which was enough for a while to support the whole mission. It was here that he compiled the first Bengali grammar and wrote tracts in that language which constituted its first prose literature. Thirty-one different translations of the Scriptures in Indian languages were also put forth by these men in the first seventeen years. This was their first and chief work, but a close second to it in importance was the education of the people of India, especially in their own and in the Indian classical languages. Before Carey had been a year in India he opened a primary school at Mudnabutti at his own cost and daily superintended it. In Serampore and in every new station as it was formed, a school was opened for non-Christian children, and by the year 1818, twenty-five years after their arrival, the Serampore brethren had founded and superintended 126 schools containing 10,000 Indian boys. They also early paid great attention to the subject of female education, and in 1826 they had 12 girls' schools in which 300 girls received an elementary secular education, and were also instructed in the Christian religion.

The Serampore missionaries very early conceived the idea, and on August 24th, 1818, had completed the plan, of establishing a Christian college, in which knowledge was to be imparted in English, Hebrew, Greek, Sanskrit, Arabic, and Chinese, and a number of the Indian vernaculars; other subjects also were to be taught, such as mathematics, medicine, jurisprudence, ethics, and theology. The Governor-General of India and the Danish governor of Serampore sanctioned the scheme, and royal support came from the king of Denmark, who granted them a valuable estate as an endowment, and better still, a royal charter of incorporation with authority to confer literary and honorary degrees. The object and methods of the college are thus explained by Dr. Marshman, in a letter to the Scottish missionary, John Wilson, of Bombay, dated September 23rd, 1834 :—

"The assertion of the founders of the college is fully justified, that their object in planning it was 'The enlightenment of India and the propagation and final establishment of the gospel therein' ...... But as to the religious character of the institution, if there be any alteration, it is that it has become even more decided........The heathen students are all under my own care in the English department, and are classed with their Christian countrymen without any distinction but what may arise from their various degrees of proficiency in all their studies not purely theological. All of them who are sufficiently advanced read and study the Scriptures two days in the week ; and all their other studies, whether in science or history, are conducted after a Christian manner. At morning worship, indeed, the Christian students alone are required to attend, and nothing either in profession or practice is required of any heathen which is inconsistent with his own faith ; but the whole controversy between Christianity and idolatry and the whole contrast between religion and irreligion are before them continually ; and we leave the result with God. What more can be necessary to make the college a religious institution?" *

The London Missionary Society started its work in India in 1798, when the Rev. Nathaniel Forsythe went out as its first representative. Some of the earliest reports of his work speak of his efforts in school work around Calcutta, and he was soon followed by Mr. May, an ardent educationalist, who devoted most of his time to the spread of education. So very successful was he in this work that at the end of 1815 he had 20 schools under his charge, with 1,651 children, of whom as many as 258 were sons of Brahmans, a remarkable thing in those times. His work received favorable notice and commend-

* Quoted by Dr. George Smith in *Life of John Wilson.*

ation from Mr. Gordon Forbes, the Commissioner of Chinsurah, and the Governor-General readily complied with the request of Mr. Forbes to aid the scheme with imperial funds, and a liberal grant of 600 rupees (then $300) a month was sanctioned. This was the first time that the government of India had given a grant-in-aid for missionary education. In one year after that the schools had increased to 30, and the children to 2,600, and the government grant also was increased to 800 rupees. As early as 1821 the L.M.S. had established five schools for girls in and around Calcutta. The foreign missionaries were also re-inforced and the work was prosecuted with great zeal along both educational and evangelistic lines; yet the results of the work during the first fifty years were very meager.

In 1804 the L.M.S. began work in South India, in Tinnevelly, and Travancore, through the eccentric but enthusiastic Ringletaube, who labored with apostolic zeal, dressed in Indian fashion, often going without coat or shoes. He trained a few Indian workers, but for the rest did nothing for the cause of education. Ringletaube left mysteriously in 1815 but two others came in 1819, and soon began to reap an abundant harvest from their predecessor's work. A theological seminary was established at Nagercoil, which sent out scores of earnest preachers, and multitudes of the people were turned to the Lord, so that in 1830 more than 4,000 had become Christians. 97 schools had also been established with 3,100 pupils. A boarding school for girls was started in Nagercoil by the missionary's wife, and girls were trained in religious and secular knowledge; and the lace making was begun for which that school afterwards became and still is famous. In 1805 the L. M. S. sent its first missionary to Madras city, but for a long time very little work was accomplished. Preaching the gospel in the streets was the method commonly employed, though in 1827 the mission had 600 Indian youths under instruction in its various schools in and around Madras.

The Society for the Propagation of the Gospel entered upon its work in India in 1820, and through its first missionary, Bishop Middleton, began a splendid scheme of higher education. A college was founded to prepare Indian Christian youths as preachers, catechists, and school teachers; also to impart useful knowledge in the English language to Hindus and Mohammedans. The foundation stone was laid the first year, still the magnificent buildings rose but slowly, and for many years the great conceptions of its founder were wholly unrealized. After sixty years of precarious existence the buildings were sold and the institution moved into more suitable quarters and locality. According to its latest report it had forty-one students in the college department, all Christians. This college, as well as Carey's great institution, was built in a very undesirable place, much too far away from any large city to be conveniently reached by those students for whom it was intended.

The Scottish Missionary Society sent its first missionary to Bombay in 1822, who proceeded at once to Bankot, sixty miles south, where within ten months he had started ten schools with over 500 pupils. He died soon after but the work was carried on by four others who came about that time, and within three years that mission had 42 schools in which 1,826 scholars received religious and secular instruction. It does not appear that many converts were made but it was a time of seed sowing and the daily lessons in the school were to bear fruit some day.

The Church Missionary Society began its work in

India in 1813. Its educational work began in October, 1818, when an Indian prince the Raja Jay Narayan presented the mission with a school in Benares, that had been in existence several years, together with a valuable endowment. The Society appointed one of its own missionaries as head master, and the school grew and prospered, and continues till this day, one of its largest and most efficient educational institutions. In Bombay the Rev. R. Kenney, sent out in 1820, early gave large attention to schools, of which within two years he had established six, with 150 scholars. In 1806 the Rev. Claudius Buchanan visited the Syrian Christians in Travancore, and relations were entered into between them and the Church of England which promised much help and reform to the old Eastern church. Three missionaries of the C.M.S. came in 1816 and began a useful work, one of them taking up an important position in the Syrian Christian College that had been established at Kottayam. An impulse was given to Christian education, higher and lower, which up to this time had been in a feeble condition.

In Tinnevelly work had been commenced by Indian catechists of the Danish mission, who made occasional excursions into this country from Tranquebar, so that from 1778 on there were Indian Christians. Then a German missionary, Joenicke, was sent to labor there, who burned with zeal in preaching and pioneer work and led great multitudes into the kingdom. By the year 1800 at least 4,000 converts had been gathered in, but nothing was done for their instruction and there were no missionaries to look after the congregations, so that many of them fell back, and the work did not prosper. In 1816 Mr. Hough, of the Church Missionary Society, arrived on the scene and brought new hope, and the work was transferred to this society. Both school work and evangelistic work were pushed with vigor, so that in four years 13 schools were established and 300 converts were received into the Christian community. In 1820 two earnest and able missionaries were sent to this field, Rev. B. Schmidt, and Rev. C. T. E. Rhenius. During the next ten years a most marvellous success attended this work. The people came by thousands from hundreds of villages, and renounced idolatry and the service of devils and put themselves under Christian instruction to learn to worship the one God. During this time 62 schools were established enrolling over 1,300 children, mostly of Christian converts.

The earliest American missionaries were the Congregationalists, whose missionary spirit was born at the famous Haystack meeting, when five young men of promise consecrated their lives to service in India. They arrived in Calcutta in 1812 but were forthwith expelled by the governor of the East India Company and so were scattered abroad. This persecution was not intended to benefit them, nevertheless it turned out for the furtherance of the gospel for it became the means of establishing new missions as widely apart as Burma, Bombay, Ceylon, and Java. Some of the earliest work in Bombay was the establishment of schools, which in five years numbered 25, in which 1,400 children of both sexes were educated; and by 1826 these had increased to 45 schools with 2,380 pupils, of whom 380 were girls. The Congregationalists also settled in the island of Ceylon, where they carried on a vigorous policy of education, for before the end of this period, in the year 1830, they had 155 schools with 6,037 pupils.

Several independent or union societies were organized during this period in the interests of Christian education in India. In 1817 the Calcutta School Book

Society was formed to provide suitable class books in various languages for use in mission schools. It soon proved an immense boon to the different missions and put a multitude of school books, both secular and religious, into circulation. In 1821 the British and Foreign School Society, with its headquarters in London, sent out the first lady educational missionary, Miss Cooke, an experienced teacher, who established 10 schools with 277 girls the first year. The Marchioness of Hastings gave her aid and patronage, and in her zeal traversed the gullies and back streets of the city where some of the schools were situated, which produced a great impression on the people of all classes. In 1824 the Ladies' Society for Female Education was established in Calcutta, with which Miss Cooke's work now became associated, and after two years, within five years of her arrival, she had 30 schools with 600 girls. In 1826 the Central Girls' School was erected, the foundation stone being laid by Lady Amherst, wife of the Governor-General. An Indian prince was also present, who had himself contributed 20,000 rupees to the undertaking, and who also spoke, thanking Lady Amherst and the other English ladies for their exertions on behalf of his country-women. In 1825 a School Book Society was formed in Bombay to further the work of missionary education. Very little work was done all this time in the remaining Presidency town, the city of Madras, excepting the labors of the L. M. S. above mentioned. The Christian Knowledge Society also conducted schools there, which in 1821 were educating 300 children.

The story presented in this chapter is of a fragmentary character, for it tells of spasmodic efforts of a few individuals, unorganized and burdened with heavy work of various kinds. There was certainly no well defined purpose in the school work carried on during this period, and though we probably have not obtained all the facts, so that the figures should be greater than they are here recorded, yet it must be borne in mind that the work was nearly all of a very elementary sort, and even, we might say, of an inferior nature. Many of the schools were no sooner formed than they were abandoned, and it would surely not be possible to say that all those enrolled in them were educated to any degree of proficiency. Still, these few facts gathered together here are significant because they represent the beginnings of a great movement. The figures recorded in this chapter, such as they are, make up a total for all India of 663 schools with 30,670 scholars.

CHAPTER II.

MISSIONARY EDUCATION: 1830—1882.

(1) *Alexander Duff; 1830—1878.*

In 1830 a young man of twenty-four years arrived in India who was destined to revolutionize missionary methods, especially with regard to education. Alexander Duff was a man born for his time. He occupies a prominent place among the missionaries of India of early pioneer days, as well as among the statesmen who founded the British Indian empire. No man with less consecration, with less enthusiasm, with less wisdom, with less courage, than Duff would have sufficed for the position he took, or could have so influenced the trend of affairs. But it is safe to say that he did not make the opportunities which came to him. At no other time in the history of India could he, or any one else, have accomplished so much for the cause in which he labored. The man and the time had most fittingly met; it remained only to choose the most suitable *place*, and Duff had received only one order from the committee that sent him out, that he should go to India but not to Calcutta. Yet on arrival he saw at once that the one place where he needed to be was Calcutta, which he called the brain of Hinduism. He resolved to plant his foot down there, among the half-million Bengalis of that city, who were eager for western knowledge, and were thirsting also for religious knowledge that would be more satisfying than their own superstitions.

We have already seen that Duff was not the first missionary to think of introducing schools into mission work ; nor was the effort of the missionaries the only one that was made for the enlightenment of the people of India. Fifty years before Duff, in 1780, Warren Hastings had founded the Madrissa or Muhammadan College in Calcutta, which was to teach the whole range of the religion of Islam, as well as the arts and sciences as worked out by Arabic scholars a thousand years before. In 1791 Jonathan Duncan did the same thing for the Hindus by establishing the Benares Sanskrit College for the purpose of cultivating their "Laws, Literature, and Religion." In 1813 the Court of Directors in London of the East India Company wrote in their despatch to the Company in India, "That a sum not less than one lakh of rupees (then $50,000) in each year shall be set apart and applied to the revival and improvement of literature ...... and for the introduction and promotion of a knowledge of the sciences among the inhabitants of the British territories of India." The Company was embarrassed with such a large sum of money, and only a part of it was used and that almost entirely for the promotion of Orientalism. In 1817 an intelligent Brahman of noble birth, the Rajah Rammohun Roy, with the help of both English and Indian friends started "The Hindu College of Calcutta," in which the English language and English literature and European sciences were to be taught. Thus we see the strange spectacle of the natives of India striving to pull down their ancient systems and teaching modern learning, and the English government doing all in its power to uphold the old and worn out superstitions.

Such was the condition of things when Duff arrived late in May, 1830 : and though this was the hottest time of all the year, he at once set out with indomitable energy and visited every missionary and mission station in and around Calcutta. There was not a school which he did not inspect; he spent hours in the thatched bamboo and wicker-work chapels, where he watched the people and the preaching, and conferred with all the workers. He returned from a six weeks tour with his mind fully made up that his own method of operations must be different from that of all his predecessors. Going up to the room of the saintly Carey, then three years before his death, he laid his plans fully before him and obtained his approval, the one authority whose opinion was best worth having: but of all the other missionaries there was not one that did not frown upon his schemes. Duff resolved in the strength of God to attempt the overthrow of a system of religion that was entrenched behind a hoary philosophy and civilization and literature of the most elaborate type, a system which till that time had remained practically untouched by the 125 years of earnest missionary effort from Ziegenbalg to Carey. Duff realized that the prevailing missionary methods had failed against the system of Brahman Hinduism. The learned and consecrated Abbe Dubois in South India had confessed the hopelessness of the task. Henry Martyn, saint and scholar, who had burned up for India, had declared that he would as soon expect to see a man rise from the dead as to see a Brahman converted to Jesus Christ. Others, such as Duff's own dear friend, Lacroix, who spent fifty years in evangelistic work largely among the higher castes, confessed the almost utter barrenness of that mode of work. It is thus that Duff himself characterizes the difference that existed between the operations hitherto employed and his own method: "While they engage in directly separating as many precious atoms from the mass as the stubborn resistance to ordinary appliances can admit, we shall, with the blessing of God devote our time and strength to the preparing of a mine, and the setting of a train, which shall one day explode and tear up the whole from its lowest depths."

What was the plan so early formed in Duff's mind that would accomplish so much for the great object he had in view ? It was to establish a system of religious education, the foremost principle of which was the reading of some portion of the Bible daily by every class, and having the same carefully expounded by Christian teachers, who aimed to impress the heart and to quicken the conscience of the pupils and sought to lead them to a living faith in God. At the same time every variety of useful knowledge would be taught, and that not only in the elementary branches but in all the higher departments of learning. He would lay the foundation of a system of education that would include all the branches of higher learning usually included in the colleges and universities of England and Europe, but in inseparable combination with the Christian faith and its doctrines, precepts, and evidences, especially in their practical bearing on life and conduct. This was perhaps not very different in plan and thought from what had been in the minds of other missionaries, particularly of Carey, when he founded the Serampore College, and of Bishop Middleton, when he founded his college on the Hooghly ; but they lacked the practical ability of carrying out their schemes, and other things also thwarted their plans.

The things which helped Alexander Duff, besides his own boundless energy and unrivalled ability as a teacher, and the fitness of the time and place, were the official toleration and personal friendship of the Governor-General, Lord William Bentinck ; and no less important, the help of the great Hindu reformer, the Rajah Rammohun Roy. Rammohun Roy, brought up in a strict Brahman home, at the age of sixteen renounced idolatry, and sought to find the true God, in Vedism, in Buddhism, in Muhammadanism. Cast out by his family and friends, he sought the society of English friends as well as the employ of the British government, and began to study the English Bible as a help to the study of English. Now he found God, and so impressed did he become with the teachings of the Bible that he even mastered Hebrew and Greek in order that he might read the original. Although never an avowed Christian and retaining till his death the rites and rights of his high caste, he did much to break down Hinduism and to build up the kingdom of God. He was greatly impressed with the young Scotchman's enthusiastic plans and expressed his approval of them. He emphatically declared that all true education must be religious and should aim not only at giving information to the mind but at developing the heart and character of the man. He approved of the Bible being taught, as it was the best book for moral instruction. He also approved of opening each day by asking God's blessing and expressed great admiration for the Lord's prayer.

Duff was thus greatly encouraged, but there still remained the difficulty of getting a suitable building in a convenient quarter of the town, for no Hindu would sell or rent him rooms for his purpose; and then there was the question of so far overcoming the prejudices of the people that they would allow their sons to attend. In both matters Rammohun Roy offered his own indispensable help, for he negotiated the plans for securing a house suitable for a school, and he was also personally present on the opening day when a few Brahman youths, the most of them his own friends and relatives, had assembled, and he explained the object of the founding of the school and smoothed the way for the missionary. Through his influence alone could these young men be induced even to take up a copy of the New Testament, whose very sight they deemed might make them Christians and put them out of caste. Every day Rammohun Roy visited the school and was present during the whole Bible lesson, encouraging the young men by his presence and aiding in the instruction.

Much of the work was elementary and was not of a kind to awaken enthusiasm except in the mind of a man who saw visions of the future. There was Alexander Duff, the student who had passed out of St. Andrews University its first scholar, its most brilliant essayist, its most eloquent debater, spending six hours a day in a hot, sultry room, surrounded by three hundred swarthy youths, teaching them the English alphabet ! O-X, ox, was the lesson of the first day, and then by the interrogatory method all that was possible was brought out concerning this familiar object. How different from the pedantic methods in vogue in the old Sanskrit schools, which drilled the memory fourteen years in the Sanskit grammar. The students were delighted, and went out into the streets pointing to an ox drawing a cart, and shouting " OX ! " at the top of their voices. They also told their friends about the strange teacher, and soon he was the talk of the town, and hundreds who applied for admission had to be turned away. Duff wisely saw that a knowledge of their own vernacular was even more important than English, and that it was in danger of being neglected if special attention were not devoted to it. Here the missionary himself joined the class and soon rivalled with the other students in their knowledge of the language. Duff was quite alone in these efforts and lived among his students despised and almost forgotten by his fellow missionaries. At the end of a year the first public examination was held in the Free Mason's Hall, presided over by Archdeacon Corrie, and attended by numerous missionaries and government officials. The boys acquitted themselves marvellously well. Their manner of answering and explaining questions that were put to them in English grammar, geography, and arithmetic, and most of all, their knowledge of the Bible, astonished the audience, so that the system and its author at once became famous.

The excitement among the inhabitants continued unabated, and Duff was pursued along the streets by boys begging to be taken into his school. Some would say: "Me good boy, Oh, take me!" Others: "Me poor boy, Oh, take me!" Others: "Me know your commandments, Thou shalt have no other gods before me,—Oh, take me!" Tickets had to be issued to those who were selected, and men stationed at the door to see that none entered besides these. Punctual and regular attendance, steady attention to Bible studies, were among the things that tested the zeal of the students, but all these conditions were met. Parents also came and listened to the exposition of the Scriptures. What an impression was made upon some who heard the truth for the first time. Reading the thirteenth chapter of First Corinthians, the description of love, which *endureth all things*, one of the young men, the very Brahman who but a few days before had risen to oppose the reading of the Bible now started from his seat, exclaiming aloud: "Oh, sir, that is too good for us! Who can act up to that?" Reading of the blessedness of him who loves and prays for his enemy, one youth was so impressed that for days and weeks he could not help crying out:—"Love your enemies ! bless them that curse you ! how beautiful ! how divine ! surely this is the truth ! "

A series of English lectures on the Christian religion was now planned by Duff and a few of his associates to be delivered in the home of one of them. The first was very well attended, but such an uproar was created in the town, and government officials and government teachers in the Sanskrit College used their influence against the missionary, so that Duff's school was for a brief time deserted and the remainder of the course could not be given. But this was only a temporary break in the work, which soon went on with redoubled vigor. The second year the lectures were again attempted, and with better success, for they were attended by a goodly number of earnest inquirers, which soon resulted in their really turning to the Lord. Said the first convert, Mohesh Chunder Ghose, before many witnesses :—" A twelve-month ago I was an atheist, a materialist, a necessitarian ; and what am I now ?—A baptized Christian. A twelve-month ago I was the most miserable of the miserable, and what am I now ?—In my own mind the happiest of the happy !" Krishna Mohun Banerjea, for some time the editor of a reform paper, was the second convert. He afterwards became an ordained minister of the Church of England. A little later, Gopeenath Nandi sought an interview with Dr. Duff in his study and burst forth in tears with the cry: " Can I be saved ? " He suffered much persecution from the members of his family and caste, but he remained steadfast, until twenty-five years later he met a martyr's death amid the captivity and bloodshed of the mutiny of 1857. Anundo Chund Mozoomdar, the youth who had been drawn to the teachings of the Sermon on The Mount (above mentioned) was the fourth convert. His father, strange to say, generously wrote to Duff to receive his persistent son, and to convert him in his own way.

But it is not our purpose now to examine in detail all these conversions that occurred in connection with Duff's educational movement. Suffice it to say that there was a tremendous awakening and upheaval, and scores of young men of the best familes joined the movement and became leaders of the Christian church in India for the next half-century. Alexander Duff had set the pace in a great work that was destined to change the face of the Indian nation. In four short years, for so soon was he compelled by ill health to leave the country, he had created a new model and given an example that was carefully studied and closely followed, not only by missionaries, but by the government educationalists, who around 1835 were shaping the course of British education in India.

We have already seen that the Court of Directors had set apart 100,000 rupees for education in India, and that this amount was being spent for the Muhammadan and Hindu colleges in Benares and Calcutta, and for the furtherance of Oriental learning. In 1833, with the renewal of the charter of the East India Company, this grant was increased to one million rupees, and now the controversy rose to great height as to what kind of education the grant was to be applied to. The following description of a sample of the science taught in the Sanskrit College is taken from Bishop Heber's account. "Under a grant ordered by Parliament on the pressure of the Christian public and administered by a Christian government, a professor lecturing on a terrestrial globe identified Mt. Meroo with the North Pole, declared that the tortoise of Hindu cosmogony supported the earth from under the South Pole, pointed to Padalon in the center of the globe, and demonstrated how the sun went round the earth every day and visited the signs of the Zodiac!" Even this was harmless compared to the obscenely idolatrous teaching that was found in government school books. For all these books were printed at government expense, and students were hired to spend years in learning the intricacies of Sanskrit grammar and such rubbish of science. Yet it was argued that the imperial grant could not lawfully be diverted to other educational purposes because it had been pledged to the promotion of Oriental learning. The Educational Committee of the government were evenly divided, five on each side: one party, including in its number Mr. H. T. Prinsep, secretary to the government, maintained that only Oriental learning should be promoted; which meant that great attention was to be paid to the acquirement of the Sanskrit, Arabic, and Persian languages, the sciences were to be taught according to the old Ptolemaic and Aristotelian methods, and the intricate and confusing systems of Hindu and Muhammadan Law were to be expounded. The other party, which included the doughty Sir Charles Trevelyan, maintained that according to the original pledge of the government not Oriental learning but "useful" learning was to be promoted; that this meant the best that could be found in all science, taught according to European methods; that the Indians themselves desired an English education; that it was in the true interests both of the people of India and of the government that the truth should be taught and not falsehood: true science, true astronomy, true metaphysics, and not false science. false astronomy, false medicine, and false metaphysics. (Strange that these things had even to be stated!) Where did Sir Charles Trevelyan get his inspiration, and where did he get his facts that helped him to fight this battle? Was it not entirely from the person and example of Duff, whose acquaintance he had made scarce a week after his arrival in 1831, when Duff's plans, his experience, his success, were accomplished facts, and for twelve months had been the talk and the imitation of many? From that hour he clung to the missionary, and became the principal link between his far-seeing practical principles on the one hand, and the coming action of the government on the other. Nearly fifty years later Trevelyan wrote on the subject:

"Our concern is with the part performed by Dr. Duff at this crisis of Indian history When he arrived in India the first marvellous results of the education given at the Hindu College had begun to appear. Newly acquired freedom had led to a state of intellectual exaltation and......the young men jumped to the conclusion that all religion was priestcraft... ..Dr. Duff clearly appreciated the new intellectual and moral power which had appeared on the field and the important use to which it might be applied in aid of the Christian cause. There was a general demand for education and he proposed to meet it by giving religious education......Whatever difficulties the government might have, the missionary societies were free to offer religious education to all who were willing to accept it. The remarkable success of the school which Dr. Duff opened at Calcutta on these principles, and the influence it had in promoting the establishment of similar institutions in other parts of India, are well known; but account must be taken also of the direct access thus gained to the future leaders of the people, and of the new respect paid to missionaries as tutors of young native chiefs and other highly considered persons. These were great and pregnant reforms, which must always give Dr. Duff a high place among the benefactors of mankind. *The indirect influence of his exertions upon the action of the government was at least equally important. The example of his success, and the stimulus given by him to the popular demand for English education entered largely into the causes which brought about the Resolution of the government of the seventh of March, 1835.*" *

---

*Quoted by Dr. George Smith, in life of Alexander Duff; Vol. I, pp. 195, 196.

Nor need we doubt Duff's own direct influence in the matter over Lord William Bentinck himself. From the time that Duff landed, when he sought his first interview with Bentinck, he had carefully expounded on many occasions his plans and views on education: and the governor in turn had always followed his arguments with interest and had been a charmed observer of his project. It was a pity, indeed that just during the greatest heat of the controversy Duff was away from India, but his influence was felt nevertheless. It fell to Macauley, who arrived in 1834 and was appointed President of the Committee of Public Instruction, to draft his famous Minute of the second of February, in which he so earnestly and eloquently set forth the cause of modern science and English education, and these views were embodied in the Governor-General's order of the seventh of March that settled the policy of public education in India. The order was to the effect that the chief aim of the educational policy should be to promote a knowledge of European literature and science, and that no new stipends should be given for the old learning, and that the printing of Oriental books should at once cease. Following this action of the government Alexander Duff wrote a pamphlet to the churches of Scotland on the "New Era of the English Language and English Literature in India," in which he explained and commended the position the government had taken. But he was not satisfied that enough had been done. The following extract from this important pamphlet is worth considering :—

"But highly as we approve of Lord W. Bentinck's enactment so far as it goes, we must in justice to our own views and to the highest and noblest cause on earth take the liberty of strongly expressing our own honest conviction that it does not go far enough. Truth is better than error in any department of knowledge, the humblest as well as the most exalted. Hence it is that we admire the moral intrepidity of the man who decreed that, in the government institutions of India, true literature and true science should henceforth be substituted in place of false literature, false science, and false religion. But we cannot but lament that no provision whatever has been made for substituting the only true religion—Christianity—in place of the false religion which our literature and science will inevitably demolish.........But because a Christian government has chosen to neglect its duty towards the religion which it is sacredly bound to uphold, is that any reason why the churches of Britain should neglect their duty too? ....If we are wise in time, we may convert the act of the Indian government into an ally and a friend. ....Wherever a government seminary is founded, which shall have the effect of battering down idolatry and superstition, there let us be prepared to plant a Christian institution that shall, through the blessing of heaven, be the instrument of rearing the beauteous superstructure of Christianity on the ruins of both." *

As to Lord Bentinck's opinion of Duff's work we have his own testimony in one of his farewell speeches, in which he spontaneously alluded to it and encouraged missionary societies to devote their efforts to education. "I would give them as an example in support of this advice the school founded exactly upon those principles, lately superintended by the estimable Mr. Duff, that has been attended with such unparalleled success." †

And this in a private letter to Duff not long after :— "I have always considered the Hindu College as one of the greatest engines of useful purpose that had been erected since our establishment in India ; but that institution, in point of usefulness, can bear no comparison with yours, in which improved education of every kind is combined with religious instruction." ‡

* Smith's Life of Duff, Vol. I, pp. 201, 202.
† Idem, p. 266. ‡ Idem p. 338.

Alexander Duff's school had grown to a college, well organized, with a carefully prepared curriculum of studies, and a staff of well-equipped teachers headed by himself and his Scottish colleagues, Dr. W. S. Mackay and others. At first, as we saw, he was alone among missionaries in this work, but he did not long remain so. He found allies not only in Calcutta but in Bombay, in Madras, and in other parts of India. Particularly celebrated are the names of other missionaries of his own church, Dr. John Wilson of Bombay, who had arrived there in 1829, and founded his college in 1832; and Dr. John Anderson, who founded a similar institution in Madras in 1837. But before turning to these we will first follow out the thread of Duff's career in Calcutta, where he arrived a second time in May, 1840, just ten years after his first arrival. The work there had not suffered during his absence, but had greatly increased by the efforts of his worthy colleagues, and so the remembrance of what he had faced ten years before, as he sailed up the Hooghly, formed a vivid contrast to what now met his eye. Even he was astonished at the outward signs of progress which ten years of English education under really enlightened British administration had brought about. A sign-board of an Indian firm of "Surgeons and Druggists" greeted him first, and showed what a change had come about since the pseudo-Orientalists had declared, only six years previous, that no Hindu would be found to study even the rudiments of the healing art through anatomy; then the Medical College, and after that the handsome English Episcopal church and parsonage, near Cornwallis Square, of which the Rev. Krishna Mohun Banerjea, LL.D., the second convert of his mission, was the honored pastor; and last of all the Assembly's new Institution and mission house, built since his departure, that were now to form his own residence and sphere of operations. The sight of these buildings, costing $30,000, contributed largely by his personal friends and partly by money given him for his own private use, greatly gladdened his heart; but better than that was the welcome accorded him by seven hundred students, who honored and loved him with true appreciation for all that his coming, ten years before, had meant to them.

Of the internal development of the work under these five spiritually consecrated and intellectually capable Scotchmen during the next fifteen years it is not our purpose to write in detail. The first attempt at normal training had not yet been made, but now systematic efforts were made by Duff and his associates, by means of lectures on pedagogy and by practical lessons in the art of teaching. Duff's own manner of teaching was significant, emphasizing the importance of clear ideas of things as contrasted with the learning of mere words. Although the study of literature was at that time probably foremost, yet the sciences were not forgotten. Mechanics, hydrostatics, pneumatics, optics, astronomy, the principles of the steam engine, etc., were taught in the college classes. A course of lectures on chemistry was also delivered, accompanied with experiments; geology was studied on account of its bearing on theology, and the students were made familiar with the use of the sextant, and other nautical and surveying instruments. "In all this, however, again as in the solitary time of his founding the mission, the intellectual was directed above all things, and excluding all other immediate ends, to the spiritual. A new creation in Christ Jesus was what the founder and his four colleagues of like spirit with himself sought to make every student, while they were sustained by the divinely given consciousness that they were working for ages yet to come, under the only Leader with whom a thousand years are as one day, against a system which would not fall, as it had not risen, in a night." *

It is important to note briefly again the relation between Duff's work and the government system of education during this time. It was a momentous period. We have noted the important decision of Lord Bentinck in 1835, which brought about such successful changes in the educational life of India. The old college under the stipendiary system had been filled with children of indigent parents, but now became crowded with numbers of the upper and middle classes, who were prepared to pay for an English education. When the Hooghly College was opened in August, 1836, 1200 names were enrolled on the first three days. There was great intellectual excitement and English schools were springing up on all sides. Nevertheless, the old party that had stood for Oriental learning felt aggrieved and saw little good in the new movement. They continued to strive, if not for the whole appropriation, for a good share of it, and a good case was made out on account of the paramount literary and philological importance of the Sanskrit and Arabic languages. Lord Auckland, then, restored to these studies the annual grant of 25,000 or 30,000 rupees, which were in course of being transferred to other departments of education. There was danger that the old Oriental methods would be revived and that English education, which had proved so successful would be starved as far as government efforts were concerned. One other mistake of Lord Auckland's was that it shelved the plan for the improvement of vernacular schools and teachers, which Lord Bentinck had sought to

* Smith's Life of Duff, Vol. I, p. 457.

encourage. At a time when many were praising the Governor-General, Duff had the courage to write a series of open letters indicting the course of error that seemed again to be favored. The following characteristic passage from one of these letters will show the tenor of them :—

"Here are two systems of education, directly opposed to each other and absolutely contradictory in their entire substance, scope, and ends. Reviewing these two systems, Lord W. Bentinck, with the straightforward bearing of British manliness and British courage in the spirit which fired the old barons of Runnymede, and with the decisive energy of uncompromising principle, thus pronounced his decision :—'Regardless of the idle clamours of interested partisanship, and fearless of all consequences, let us resolve at once to repudiate altogether what is demonstrably injurious, because demonstrably false, and let us cleave to and exclusively promote that which is demonstrably beneficial, because demonstrably true.' Reviewing the very same system, my Lord Auckland, with what looks very like the tortuous bearing of Machiavellian policy, in the spirit of shrinking timidity, which heretofore has compromised the success of the best laid schemes, and with Proteus-like facility of temporizing expediency, thus enunciates his contrary verdict :—'Fearful of offending any party, wishing to please all, and anxious to purchase peace at any price, let us,—dropping all minor distinctions between old and new, good and bad, right and wrong,—let us at once resolve to embrace and patronize both alike.' In a word, 'Let us,' says Lord W. Bentinck, 'disendow error and endow only truth.' 'Let us,' replies Lord Auckland, 're-endow error, and continue the endowment of truth too.'" *

In 1844 a resolution was promulgated by Lord Hardinge, which was important in its bearings on missionary education in that for the first time the value of Christian and independent colleges and schools was officially recognized, and from henceforth they as well as government schools were invited to present their students as candidates for civil service examinations. A great impetus was thus given to education of all kinds, reaching down to

* Quoted in Smith's Life of Duff.

the lowest form, for the order directed that even in the selection of persons to fill the lowest offices under Government, "A man who can read and write be preferred to one who cannot."

But the most far reaching and beneficial of enactments is yet to be dealt with: that known as the Halifax Despatch of 1854. Every twenty years the East India Company's charter was subject to renewal and it had become customary to look for important revision in such a vital matter as education. We have seen what the charters of 1813 and 1833 produced in this way. In 1853, previous to the renewal of the Company's charter, the Lords' Committee in London sought expert evidence on the subject of education in India, and among the men whose testimony was taken were Sir Charles Trevelyan, Macaulay, Prof. H. H. Wilson, Dr. Marshman, (son of the missionary), John Stuart Mill, and Alexander Duff. Among the members of the Lords' Committee were men of Indian experience, such as Ellenborough, Tweedale, and Elphinstone; and among the Commons' Committee we note the names of Palmerston, Gladstone, and Disraeli. For three days Duff was under examination, first on the whole subject of the secular administration, but at greater length on the educational needs. There were men on the examining committee who sympathised with his aims and who followed along his own lines, but there were those who were decidedly hostile and were determined by cross fire to shake his evidence. In answer to the invitation of Lord Stanley of Alderley to state what he would propose the Government should do towards the further improvement of education in India, Duff made reply as follows:—

"Fall back on the resolutions of Lord William Bentinck, which, without damaging or interfering with the existing vested rights of anyone, would lead to the gradual abolition of these Oriental colleges as seminaries for the educational training of the natives, and thus liberate the funds so wastefully lavished upon them for the purposes of a sound and healthful education throughout the land. If the learned Oriental languages are to be taught at all they ought to be taught simply as languages, with a practical view towards the enrichment of the vernacular tongues, and the raising up of a superior class of vernacular translators and teachers......Then, secondly, the time has come when, in places like Calcutta and Bombay, the Government might very well relinquish its pecuniary control over primary education. The demand is in these places so great for the higher English education that, were a test or criterion of scholarship established for admission to the colleges, the natives would be found both able and willing in sufficient numbers to qualify themselves......Thirdly, the time has come when, more especially at the Presidency seats, lectureships on high professional subjects, such as law and civil engineering, should be established, on such a free and unrestricted footing as to admit of the attendance of qualified students from all institutions, government, missionary, and others......The time has also come in Calcutta, at least, when, with comparatively little additional expense to Government, a university might be established, somewhat after the general model of the London University, with a sufficient number of faculties, constituted on so wide a basis, as to embrace within the range of its stimulating and fostering influence whatever sound, invigorating, purifying, elevating studies may be carried on in both government and non-government institutions......The time has now come when, in the estimation even of many who formerly thought otherwise, the Government might with the greatest propriety and advantage act on the principle recommended in the minute by Lord Tweedale, dated August, 1846. That principle, for very strong and weighty reasons set forth in the minute itself, is to allow the Bible to be introduced as a class-book into the English classes of government institutions, under the express and positive proviso that attendance on any class, at the hour when it was taught should be left entirely optional .....Lastly the Government ought to extend its aid to all other institutions, by whomsoever originated and supported, where a sound general education is communicated......Without directly trenching on the peculiar religious convictions or prejudices of any party, the government educational funds would have the effect of extending and multiplying tenfold really useful schools and seminaries, and of thus more rapidly and widely diffusing the benefits of an enlightened education among the masses of the people." *

These views received independent support from Sir Charles Trevelyan a few days afterwards. When asked about the conversion of India he replied:

"Many persons mistake the way in which the conversion of India will be brought about. I believe it will take place at last wholesale. The country will have Christian instruction infused into it in every way by direct missionary education, and indirectly through books of various kinds, through the public papers, and in all conceivable ways in which knowledge is communicated. Then at last, when society is completely saturated with Christian knowledge, and public opinion has taken a decided turn that way, they will come over by thousands." *

After the evidence was all received Dr. Duff and Dr. Marshman worked out the educational portion of their statements in a form which Lord Halifax, President of the Board of Control, through his private secretary, embodied in a state paper. That was sent out to the Marquis of Dalhousie as the memorable Despatch of the 9th July, 1854, signed by ten directors of the East India Company. The celebrated Despatch, which was thus the outcome of long years of investigation and experiment and agitation, has well been called the Great Charter of Indian education, on which the whole of the immense system now in existence is based. It has never been recalled or superseded, but on the contrary, has been reaffirmed in many successive government orders, even as late as the 11th March, 1904. It fills twenty-two finely printed octavo pages, of which the following extracts are of permanent interest to the subject of missionary education.

"It appears to us that the present time, when by an Act of the Imperial Legislature the responsible trust of the Govern-

* Quoted in Smith's Life of Duff,

ment of India has again been placed in our hands, is peculiarly suitable for the review of the progress which has already been made, the supply of existing deficiencies and the adoption of such improvements as may be best calculated to secure the ultimate benefit of the people committed to our charge. Among many subjects of importance, none can have a stronger claim to our attention than that of education. It is one of our most sacred duties......We have, moreover, always looked upon the encouragement of education as peculiarly important, because calculated not only to produce a higher degree of intellectual fitness, but to raise the moral character of those who partake of its advantages......

We must emphatically declare that the education which we desire to see extended in India is that which has for its object the diffusion of the improved arts, science, philosophy, and literature of Europe. The systems of science and philosophy which form the learning of the East abound with grave errors, and Eastern literature is at best very deficient as regards all modern discovery and improvements.........We do not wish to diminish the opportunities which are now afforded, in special institutions, for the study of Sanskrit, Arabic, and Persian literature, or for the cultivation of those languages, which may be called the classical languages of India. An acquaintance with the works contained in them is valuable for historical and antiquarian purposes,.........and is also of great importance for the critical cultivation and improvement of the vernacular languages of India.

We have next to consider......the medium through which knowledge is to be conveyed to the people of India. It has hitherto been necessary......for those who desired a liberal education, to begin by the mastery of the English language as a key to the literature of Europe ; and a knowledge of English will always be essential to those natives of India who aspire to a high order of education.........It is neither our aim nor desire to substitute the English language for the vernacular dialects of the country. We have always been most sensible of the importance of the use of the languages which alone are understood by the great mass of the population......It is indispensable, therefore, that in any general system of education the study of them should be assiduously attended to.........We look, therefore, to the English language and to the vernacular languages of India together, as the *media* for the diffusion of European knowledge, and it is our desire to see them cultivated together in all schools in India of a sufficiently high class to maintain a school master possessing the requisite qualifications.........

The rapid spread of a liberal education among the natives of India, the high attainments shown by the native candidates for government scholarships, and by native students in private institutions, the success of the Medical Colleges, and the requirements of an increasing European and Anglo-Indian population, have led us to the conclusion that the time is now arrived for the establishment of Universities in India......The Council of Education took the London University as their model.

The examinations for deg ees will not include any subjects connected with religious belief......As in England......so in India, institutions conducted by all denominations of Christians, Hindus, Muhammadans, Parsees, Sikhs, Buddhists, Jains, or any other religious persuasions, may be affiliated to the universities, if they are found to afford the requisite course of study, and can be depended upon for the certificates of conduct which will be required......It would greatly encourage the cultivation of the vernacular languages of India that professorships should be founded for those languages, and perhaps, also for Sanskrit, Arabic, and Persian......The grammar of these languages, and their application to the improvement of the spoken languages of the country, are the points to which the attention of these professors should be mainly directed ; and there will be ample field for their labors unconnected with any instruction in the tenets of the Hindu or Muhammadan religions. We should refuse to sanction any such teaching, as directly opposed to the principle of religious neutrality to which we have always adhered.........

We propose, therefore, that the Council of Education at Calcutta, and the Board of Education at Bombay, with some additional members to be named by Government, shall constitute the Senate of the University at each of those Presidencies. The additional members should be so selected as to give all those who represent the different systems of education which will be carried on in the affiliated institutions—including natives of India, of all religious persuasions, who possess the confidence of the native communities—a fair voice in the Senates.........

Our attention should now be directed to a consideration, if possible, still more important, and one which has been hitherto, we are bound to admit, too much neglected; namely, how useful and practical knowledge, suited to every station in life, may be best conveyed to the great mass of the people......We desire to see the active measures of Government more especially directed, for the future, to this object.........

In so far as the noble exertions of societies of Christians of all denominations to guide the natives of India in the way of religious truth, and to instruct uncivilised races, such as those found in Assam, in the Cossya, Garrow, and Rajamehal Hills, and in various districts of Central and Southern India, have been accompanied in their educational establishments, by the diffusion of improved knowledge, they have largely contributed to the spread of that education which it is our object to promote.

The consideration of the impossibility of Government alone doing all that must be done in order to provide adequate means for the education of the natives of India...has led us to the natural conclusion that the most effectual method of providing for the wants of India in this respect will be to combine with the agency of Government the aid which may be derived from the exertions and liberality of the educated and wealthy natives of India, and of other benevolent persons. We have, therefore, resolved to adopt in India the system of grants-in-aid and we confidently anticipate a far more rapid progress of education ;......while it possesses the additional advantage of fostering a spirit of reliance upon local exertions. The system of grants-in-aid which we propose to establish in India, will be based on an entire abstinence from interference with the religious instruction conveyed in the schools assisted. Aid will be given to all schools which impart a good secular education...... In their periodical inspections, *no notice whatsoever* should be taken by them of the religious doctrines which may be taught in any school.........

We look forward to the time when any general system of education entirely provided by Government may be discontinued, with the gradual advance of the system of grants-in-aid, and when many of the existing government institutions, especially those of the higher order, may be safely closed, or transferred to the management of local bodies......

Considerable misapprehension appears to exist as to our views with respect to religious instruction in government institutions.

Those institutions were founded for the benefit of the whole population of India; and, in order to effect their object, it was, and is, indispensable that the education conveyed in them should be exclusively secular. The Bible is, we understand, placed in the libraries of the colleges and schools, and the pupils are able freely to consult it. This is as it should be; and, moreover, we have no desire to prevent, or discourage, any explanations which the pupils may, of their own free will, ask from the masters upon the subject of the Christian religion, provided that such information be given out of school hours. Such instruction being entirely voluntary on both sides, it is necessary, in order to prevent the slightest suspicion of an intention on our part to make use of the influence of Government for the purpose of proselytism, that no notice shall be taken of it by the inspectors in their periodical visits.........

In Madras, where little has yet been done by Government to promote the education of the mass of the people, we can only remark with satisfaction that the educational efforts of Christian missionaries have been more successful among the Tamil population than in any other part of India." *

* The Educational Policy of the State of India, pp. i—xxii.

CHAPTER II. (CONTINUED).

MISSIONARY EDUCATION : 1830-1882.

---

(2) *The Growth and Extension of Missionary Education.*

We have thus far considered this period especially as centered in the life of its greatest representative, but we have also had occasion to allude to the work of others, who were taught by his methods and encouraged by his example and inspired by his enthusiasm. Alone he could not have accomplished even all the work that directly grew under his hands, nor could he have influenced the state system of education as he did. In the celebrated Despatch, as we have seen, the work particularly of the Madras missionaries was commended, but all through India during this period the work of missionary education grew and spread and was given a more definite aim than it had during the earlier period. The earliest and most important part in this movement was borne by two missionaries of the same church as Dr. Duff, namely, John Wilson of Bombay and John Anderson of Madras. John Wilson arrived in Bombay in 1829, a year before Duff arrived in Calcutta, and began a work there with the same zeal and enthusiasm that we saw characterized his brother Scot in Calcutta. He was more distinguished than Duff for his knowledge of Oriental literature and language and thought, and was remarkably powerful in his controversies with the Hindus, Parsees, and Jews of Bombay. Mrs. Wilson organized female schools almost immediately on their arrival. Vernacular schools had also been established by the American Congregationalists but it remained for the Scottish missionary to establish the first English school in 1834. The Baptist Serampore College and Duff's institution in Calcutta were his models, which he studied with great care. Wilson believed in the importance of emphasizing the study of the vernacular and classical languages of India as well as English, just as Duff had done before. The subjects and the textbooks of his college were those of the Scottish Universities. not excluding Greek and Hebrew. He himself lectured on the Evidences of Christianity, Biblical Criticism, and Systematic Divinity.

The college in Bombay did not create such a stir as Duff's in Calcutta, nor did it grow so rapidly in numbers. At the end of six years we find 155 students, of whom 33 were Christians and 78 Hindus, the remainder Jews and Muhammadans. Young Bombay was not the same as young Bengal, and the personality of the missionary may have had something to do with it. But the spiritual fruit of Wilson's institution was almost as remarkable. Four years after Wilson had come to Bombay the Zoroastrian controversialists had taunted him with the assertion that the conversion of a Parsee was not to be dreamed of; but five years after that three Parsee students, the first fruits of the college work, became Christians and were baptized. This was a terrible shock to the community. All the Parsee boys were at once withdrawn from all mission schools in Bombay, and a decree was passed by the heads of the Parsee body forbidding any parent or guardian, under pain of utter outlawry from the Parsee religion and society, ever to send a child to such institutions. Also funds were forthwith subscribed to establish an opposition school. No missionary would fail to sympathize with these people in their feelings; and these divisions that come in families because of Jesus Christ, that cause them to cast out and scorn those whom they once tenderly loved, are heart rending, and if it were not the way pointed out by the Master himself, no one would have the heart to be a partner in or an occasion of such a state of things. Moreover, few missionaries lament efforts to which people are stirred up in self-defence, shown often as in the above mentioned case, by building schools of their own. It is much better that they should build schools than temples, and there is room for all the schools they can build. One of the converts above mentioned was Dhanjibhai Nauroji, a young man of great promise, who afterwards visited Edinburgh and finished his education there. He was then ordained to the gospel ministry and was for many years one of the most prominent Indian members of the Mission.

We must not forget the important part that John Wilson played in the legislation of 1853-1857. The following extracts from a letter that he wrote to the Committee of the church at home, dated May 16th, 1855, indicate his attitude towards the Education Despatch that had just been promulgated:

"We rejoice to learn that our Committee at home are disposed to concur in our co-operation with Government in carrying its provisions into effect in so far as they may be found to apply to our missionary establishments. The issue of the Despatch constitutes a new and promising epoch in connection with the intellectual and moral enlightenment of this great country. It fully recognizes important principles for which we have long and strenuously contended in this Presidency. It forms a discriminative and judicious estimate of the comparative claims of the vernacular and learned languages of India and of English as media of instruction. It makes a very cordial acknowledgement of the benefits derived by India from the missionary enterprise. It makes the Bible accessible for purposes of consultation to inquisitive youths within the walls of the government seminaries. It permits the communication to them at extra hours of Christian instruction, voluntarily imparted and voluntarily received. It promises certain grants in aid of secular instruction. ......The effects of the Despatch on missionary operations will be to open a wide field to the work of our Bible and Tract societies and missionary presses.......It will aid missionaries in that department of their labors which embraces secular knowledge. But missionaries and their supporters must vow before God and man not to dilute or diminish their religious instruction in their seminaries on this account." *

In a letter which Dr. Wilson wrote to Dr. Duff in 1863 he refers thus to what had been accomplished by the exertions of the Bombay missionaries to influence the state curriculum:

"Had it not been for the most strenuous and almost self-destroying efforts and exertions which I made from day to day, during the first discussion of the by-laws, there would have been no recognition in them as subjects of study, of Moral Philosophy, of Jewish History, and of Evidences of Christianity, in the case of undergraduates electing them......For our systematic Bible reading and lecturing we can maintain a due place, by insisting on the conditions of our missionary institutions. It is a fact that the eagerness for graduation is a temptation to many young men to confine their attention to the studies prescribed by the Universities, but what would be the consequences if, instead of opposing that temptation we were to withdraw from the arena? What would be the character of the Universities themselves?" †

Dr. Wilson's position as acknowledged by Government may be seen further in the fact that, when the Bombay University was founded he was at once elected as a member of its Senate. He also became a member of the Syndicate of studies, Dean of the Faculty of Arts,

* Quoted by Dr. Geo. Smith: Life of John Wilson. p. 531.

† Idem p. 535.

and University Examiner in Sanskrit, Persian, Hebrew, Marathi, Goojarati, Hindustani, and once held the place of Vice-Chancellor of the University.

While Duff was involuntarily absent from Calcutta, from 1835 to 1839, he was busily engaged in Scotland in securing the interest of that people, which has ever since continued, and which has caused so many of her sons to give themselves to educational work in India. Though sick with a raging fever Duff rose from his bed and went to the Assembly's meeting in Edinburgh, and there delivered his first address, which thrilled his audience A report of this speech fell into the hands of John Anderson, a student, then sick in bed, which so aroused his enthusiasm that he forthwith resolved, as soon as he might recover, to go to India. He arrived in Madras the next year and there, in the third largest city of India, opened St. Andrew's school with 59 pupils, which was destined to become the largest Christian institution not only in India but in all Asia, the Madras Christian College. In his prospectus Mr. Anderson said: "The ultimate object is a normal seminary in which native teachers and preachers may be trained to convey to their benighted countrymen the benefits of a sound education and the blessings of the gospel of Christ." In two months the numbers rose to 180. The school was intended for high caste Hindus, but one morning three pariah boys presented themselves under the guise of Brahmans and were taken in. Their identity was soon discovered but Mr. Anderson refused to send them away, and one hundred Brahmans at once left the school. They came back, however, and soon the school was more prosperous than ever. About this time Anderson wrote: "Our greatest trial now is that we do not see the souls over whom we yearn converted to God. Our hearts begin to yearn for the first ripe fruits." But they had not much longer to wait. In June, 1841, two Brahman youths accepted Christ and were baptized. The number of students was reduced from 400 to 70. The relatives of the young men appealed to the court, but they were found to be of full age and declared capable of deciding for themselves in matters of religion. The father of one of the boys upbraided one of the judges, himself a Brahman, because he had concurred in the decision of his English colleagues. He replied: "Mr. Anderson is an honest man; he told you from the beginning that conversion was his object, yet you placed your son under his instruction." A third was baptized after a few weeks, and after some months, when the students had mostly come back, another Brahman student was converted, and again the school was emptied.

Bishop Caldwell, who visited Madras about this time, left some of his impressions of Anderson in his Reminiscences: "One of his chief characteristics was his almost womanly tenderness and affection towards his students, which was one of the things that conduced to the great number of conversions of the educated young men with which his work was marked. Throughout the Presidency of Madras for many years the name of John Anderson and the fame and influence of what was called Anderson's school were like household words."

Mrs. Braidwood, the wife of one of the missionaries sent out in connection with the college, opened a school for Brahman girls in her own home. The result of this work likewise was the conversion of eight of them, but the school was completely swept away for a time. The results of the first twelve years of the educational work of Anderson and his colleagues in Madras were 50 teachers trained, 7000 Hindu and Muhammadan students instructed, 1000 girls in the schools, 36 believers baptized, three ordained preachers and five others almost ready for the same work. By the year 1858, 93 adults had received the rite of baptism, and the conversion of these persons was to be traced under God mainly to the teaching and preaching of the truth in the institution.

Brief mention must be made of another Scotchman, John Murdoch, who arrived in India in 1844 and spent sixty years in her service, chiefly in the production and distribution of Christian school books and other literature in English and also in the various vernaculars throughout India. He founded the South India Christian School Book Society, which was afterwards merged into the Christian Vernacular Education Society, of which he was the first travelling agent and Indian secretary, and till his death in 1904 he remained the very soul of its existence. At the age of eighty-five years he was still busy, and while with pen in hand he was correcting a proof of one of his writings, death called him painlessly away. The Society was formed by Christian people in England as a memorial of the Indian Mutiny, and a large Memorial Hall was erected in Madras, as a token of gratitude for deliverance and also of forgiveness of their enemies. The two principal objects of the Society were the training of Indian masters for the instruction of Indian children, and the production of a Christian literature in the chief languages of India. The great denominations of England all joined in this great movement. Three training institutions were founded in different parts of India, in which more than 1200 teachers were trained. This work was abandoned about the year 1883 because these institutions ultimately became the training colleges of the missions in whose fields they were situated. The publication of school books and other Christian literature proved a most useful undertaking. During the first ten years of its existence 250 different works were published in fourteen languages, and the number of copies issued was three million. The society's books were used in the schools of twenty missionary societies, and fifty book depôts had been opened in the most important cities of India. Bringing this history up to the present date, it is not possible to give the total circulation of school books since the formation of the society. The total circulation of all its publications, by the Madras branch alone, from 1859 to 1906, amounted to over 21,000,000 copies, of which three-fourths are estimated to have been school books. In addition, there were many books issued by the northern branches in Marathi, Urdu, Hindi, etc., of which particulars are not available. More than two million school books were issued by the Madras branch during the last three years. These books consist of several sets of Readers in English and in the vernaculars, also Dictionaries, Geographies, Grammars, Histories, and scientific text-books. For the most part they are well written, and printed and bound in good style, and sold at a very cheap price. The last Decennial Missionary Conference of all India, Madras, 1902, called favorable attention to the Society's school publications, and there is no doubt as to the great help that this society affords to missionaries of all denominations. It remains to be noted that in 1891 the name of the Society was changed to the Christian Literature Society. *

* One of the many valuable pamphlets prepared by Dr. Murdoch is his Report on Theological Education in India, containing an account of nearly all the important theological institutions of various denominations in India, together with a synopsis of the courses of studies followed in each of them and other useful information, and a helpful discussion of the many problems and needs connected with this work of training Indian Christian preachers.

It is of course impossible to trace the history of each man henceforth, who has been engaged in education in India, or even to note the birth and progress of the different educational institutions that were established by various denominations in all parts of India during this period. While there were eight British societies and two American societies that had begun mission work in India before 1830, during the period from 1830 to 1882 fourteen additional British societies, fifteen additional American societies, eight Continental societies, and six International societies added their forces, a grand total of fifty-three societies. (A society usually corresponds to a "denomination" at home, though some societies are interdenominational, such as the Y.M.C.A.)

The American societies devoted most of their attention to more directly evangelistic or preaching work, some of them very strongly declaring themselves for a long time exclusively in favor of that mode. The American Congregationalists, after devoting much time and energy during the first half of the century to educational work, in their three fields, suddenly by the advice of a deputation sent from America, withdrew from these efforts and for a long time did practically nothing for the education of non-Christian children, and nothing at all for English education. In addition to preaching they very early established boarding schools for Christian boys and girls and training schools for educating Indian preachers and catechists, the one founded at Madura in 1842 remaining to the present time one of the strongest theological seminaries in the land. The Arcot Mission of the Dutch Reformed church was established in 1853 by the Scudder brothers and for many years was particularly strong in the number of its missionaries who were distinguished preachers in the vernacular. The American Baptists, who commenced their labors in India proper in 1836, devoted themselves almost wholly to preaching the Word in the language of the people over a wide expanse of territory. The American Methodists gave great prominence to Sunday-schools, but perhaps their most noteworthy institution established during this time was the Theological Seminary at Bareilly, one of the best and largest of its kind, which has sent out hundreds of well-trained Christian workers. Their emphasis, needless to say, was placed on preaching. This was also the case with the Presbyterians, yet mention should be made of an interesting experiment in school work made by them at this time. In 1859 they established a high grade institution for Indian Christian girls at Dehra Doon, in the North West Provinces, which has been considered the most ambitious project of the kind in India, having aims much surpassing the ordinary female boarding and training schools that are so numerous. The school is designed to furnish a home for the girls and they are brought under the same roof with the American missionaries, who try to take the place of parents to them. The girls themselves do all the domestic work of the institution, and live together as sisters, the older ones looking after the studies and personal habits of the younger. The highest possible intellectual culture, both in the vernacular and especially in English, is also given them, and they are trained for the university examinations. This institution has the honor of having sent up the first female candidate for the university examinations in all India. The underlying motive is of course moral and spiritual, and the girls are led to Christ and to a life of Christian virtue. The school has been a pronounced success, and Christian parents of all denominations in the North West Provinces and the Punjab have sent their daughters to be educated there, paying high fees for the privilege.

The general position of the American societies on missionary educational work in India can perhaps be explained by the fact that the people of India were so far removed and were regarded only in the light of unevangelized souls in the darkness of "heathenism," whose main if not sole need was the gospel of Jesus Christ. To British Christians, on the other hand, India was a part of the British realm, and its people were fellow subjects of the queen, and their intellectual enlightenment was therefore of greater interest to them. Even to-day there are people who cannot understand how the American people have any responsibility either for evangelizing or educating the "heathen" of India. An English writer on mission work in India in 1881 bears this striking testimony to the work of American missionaries :—

> "In the judgment of the writer, acknowledgments have never been sufficiently made of the spontaneous and entirely disinterested zeal and liberality of our Western cousins in planting missions at great expense in various parts of India, and in taking part with English missionaries, and, we may add, with the British Government likewise, in the generous endeavor to enlighten and elevate its ignorant and degraded races. Their missions are well organized, are conducted with great ability and spirit, and will favorably compare with some of the best English missions." *

Turning, then, to the English societies it may be said that to the Church of Scotland, split into two parts in 1843, belongs the honor all through this period of maintaining the greatest number, and the most efficient schools, especially of high grade. We regret to note that the first one in the field, the Baptist Missionary Society, did not keep up its educational policy with any

* Sherring : History of Protestant Missions in India. p. 185.

vigor during this period, nor in fact, up to the present time. The noted Serampore College, the first Protestant mission college in India dwindled into comparative insignificance. It has long ceased to be a regular Arts college and is now a training school for Christian workers with but twenty students.* Not only with regard to this institution, but throughout their work this society relaxed its educational efforts. This was the result of a policy introduced by one of the secretaries who visited their missions in 1855, at whose suggestion their schools were closed and attention was given to preaching. The result of this exclusive method has not been encouraging and in twenty-five years their churches witnessed little growth either in numbers or in influence. The London Missionary Society suffered during this period and ever since from too great a scattering of their forces. They maintained one of the finest educational institutions in Calcutta, begun in 1837 and in 1882 having 904 students and scholars. In 1853 they built a massive and imposing building there at a cost of $34,000. Besides this the L.M.S. had high schools at Bellary and Vizagapatam. The Church Missionary Society always carried on some of the strongest missions in India and their devotion to education was second only to that of the Scottish societies. In Calcutta and its vicinity for many years they devoted much attention to lower schools, and some of their ablest missionaries gave much time to their

---

* Since the above was written an effort has been made to raise the status of the Serampore College according to the original intentions of its founders. A large scheme has been proposed by the present principal, the Rev. Dr. Howells, of making it a Christian university with an endowment of $1,000,000—and the plan has been approved by a committee representative of all the Baptist Missions working in India, which met at Serampore in March, 1908.

development. But it was long felt that with the advancement of education in Calcutta the mission ought to have an institution of its own, and in 1864 a large fund left by Bishop Wilson was made available for this purpose, and the Cathedral Mission College was established. Commodious buildings were erected on the site where Duff had lived and under able principals for a long time a high grade of work was maintained. But the difficulty of securing missionaries who were competent for this peculiar method of work and also sincerely devoted to it, seemed to be insuperable, and in 1880 that college was converted into a theological training institution. The Committee of the C.M.S. had not changed their opinion as to the great value of this form of mission work but "They did not feel justified in expending missionary money in providing collegiate education which they could not permeate with Christian teaching, owing to the lack of an adequate staff of missionary professors." Mention has already been made of the Jay Narayan's College in Benares: there are two other important institutions that deserve notice, Noble College, at Masulipatam, and St. John's College, at Agra. The former was opened in 1843 with two pupils by the Rev. R. T. Noble, who continued in charge for more than twenty years and under whose wise direction the school grew steadily till at the time of his death it reached an attendance of 300, and was then made into a college. Like other institutions of its kind it was several times emptied on account of conversions, and it suffered much opposition in consequence. It is to-day one of the strongest of the affiliated colleges of the Madras University. St. John's College was established in 1850 by an influential body of lay members of the Church of England living in India, under the Presidency of Sir William Muir. It was founded for the education of the higher classes of Indian young men upon strictly Christian principles, to create a higher moral and spiritual tone among these classes.

Much more could be said in detail of the educational work of the various societies, but we must conclude this section with a general characterization of this department of missionary labor during this period. Much progress was made during these fifty years, not only during the first half, under the great stimulus given to it by Dr. Duff, but also during the latter half, notwithstanding the fact that some missions withdrew from active participation in the work. The number of those taught increased from 30,000 in 1830 to nearly 100,000 in 1855, and this number was again more than doubled in the next twenty-five years, being increased to 241,646. A fifth of these, nearly 50,000, were in colleges and high schools, and missionaries now taught one-sixth of all scholars in secondary schools. The social position of many of the scholars in regard to caste did not differ greatly any more from that of the scholars of the state schools. Yet the missionaries had a much larger number of Christian and low-caste children, especially in elementary schools. The two terms are not convertible, yet it remains true that the large majority of Christians have come from the low castes, and that this class, Christian and non-Christian, owes a great debt of gratitude to the missionaries, who almost alone have concerned themselves about their intellectual welfare.

The growing number of girls educated is a most significant feature. It is difficult to estimate how many girls were educated in mission schools before 1830, probably not more than 2000. This number had risen to over 13,000 in 1855, while at that time not a single girl had yet found entrance to any state or native school. In 1882 the number of girls in mission schools had again increased more than five-fold to over 72,000. The improvement in the quality of instruction and in the kind of girls also that were taught is still more remarkable. Formerly, even up to 1855, they were mainly the children of the lowest castes and of the very poor; but now the highest castes and the wealthy sent their girls to mission schools. Moreover, a system of Zenana teaching had been begun, by which missionary ladies had gained admission to thousands of Hindu and Muhammadan homes, teaching all manner of useful subjects, including needle work and music. "In 1882 it was calculated that about 9000 women in all India were being taught on this system at their own homes." *

The character of all missionary education during this period was gradually raised, and according to the impulse given it by Dr. Duff was thoroughly and avowedly Christian. The Bible was regularly read, many of the Readers were saturated with Christian ideas, and the best books on the evidences of Christianity were studied. Under the system of state aid, inaugurated by the Despatch of 1854, by which large sums of money were devoted by Government to the assistance of private efforts in education, the missionaries were able to develop that side of their work at a comparatively small expense. Government supervision and partial control tended to make their work better systematized, and excepting the distinctly Christian instruction, the two systems of state and missionary education tended to become more and more like each other.

---

* Thomas: British Education in India.

CHAPTER III.

THE EDUCATION COMMISSION OF 1882-1883.

We come now to consider an important movement as related to Missionary Education. We have seen what part Dr. Duff and other missionaries had in bringing about the legislation of 1854, and what provision was made in the great Despatch for so-called aided education. The chief purposes of the Despatch were that the great masses of the people should receive the first care of Government, and that especially in secondary and higher education the state should not carry on its work directly but should foster private efforts by the grant-in-aid system. It was evident to many, who were interested in education in India during the period following this Despatch, that neither the spirit nor the letter of it was being carried out by the state educational authorities. Slowly an agitation arose at the instance largely of the missionaries, alleging unfairness in various ways in the treatment that aided education received at the hands of the department of education.

In order to collect information about the real condition of things and also to bring strong pressure to bear on the authorities both in India and in England, a General Council on Education in India was formed in 1878 with the Rev. James Johnston as secretary, and containing further such names as the Earl of Shaftesbury and Lord Halifax, the author of the Despatch of 1854.

Some of the chief points of grievance and of criticism were the following :—

(1) A great advance had actually been made in the public expenditure on higher education, while only a comparatively small increase had been made in public expenditure on primary education, so that at the close of the period the amounts granted by Government for higher education and primary education were just about equal. It was estimated that about £ 70,000 in a total expenditure of a little over a million sterling was being diverted from primary and middle education for the benefit of high schools and colleges.

(2) It was found that far from withdrawing from direct efforts in higher education the number of government colleges was more than doubled ; and to this was added a fact of considerable weight that the state schools were very much more expensive than aided ones, so that it cost the state nearly eight times as much to educate a student in one of its own institutions as in an aided school.

(3) It began to be seen that the education of the masses was not keeping pace with the increase of the population. For while, during the previous ten years, there had been a yearly increase of about 70,000 in all the schools, the number of children of school age had increased annually by over 200,000 ; so that education instead of gaining ground, was actually falling behind at the rate of 130,000 children every year, and the number of illiterates was constantly increasing.

(4) It appeared that the system of grants-in-aid had not received the encouragement which it deserved, for though the authorities had contemplated that aided education should increase and public education decrease,

it was found at the end of this period that, in the case of primary education, while in Bengal, Assam, and the Madras Presidency there was a fair number of aided schools, on the other hand, in the Central Provinces only one-third of primary education was aided, in the Punjab only one-sixth, in the North West Provinces only one-thirteenth, and in the Bombay Presidency only one twenty-fourth. In the case of secondary and collegiate education matters were even worse.

(5). Lastly, somewhat more partisan grievances were alleged by the missionaries as to unfair treatment accorded to them. The government scholarships were not tenable in their schools but only in state schools, and thus their best scholars were drawn away. The internal discipline of their schools was unwarrantably interfered with, and in some cases they were compelled to make use of books of which they entirely disapproved. Unwelcome regulations as to fees, promotions, and salaries were pressed upon them. Their grants were cut down without notice, and sometimes the grant-in-aid rules were unduly rigorous. Not seldom the government officials, inspectors, etc., were openly unfair to them in examinations. The principle of the Despatch, that where an adequate aided school existed no state school should be introduced, had been repeatedly violated. By the methods of inspection and examination a peculiar system of cramming had been fostered, damaging alike to state schools and to others, which made it particularly difficult for missionaries to provide even a slight amount of religious teaching. There was also a strong general opinion expressed against state schools, in that while destroying the native religions, they provided nothing in their place, and so were the cause of irreligion and consequent immorality so commonly springing up in India.

Now it was not, as was sometimes alleged by those who represented state education, that the missionaries desired the abolition of state schools in order that they themselves might control the whole of education. They strove rather for a transference of government schools to native authorities, and for a fair and generous carrying out of the grant-in-aid system, and for a greater emphasis on religious teaching even in state schools.

The agitation bore fruit in the appointment by the Government of India, in February, 1882, of an Education Commission, "To enquire into the existing state of Public Instruction, and to suggest means for furthering the system on a popular basis." Sir William W. Hunter, LL.D., C.I.E., a member of the Viceroy's Legislative Council, and a high authority on all Indian affairs, was appointed president of the Commission, which consisted of twenty-one members representing fairly the views of all parties concerned, "not only of the Educational Department, and of the local Executive of the different Provinces, but also of the educated native community and of the missionary bodies." * In appointing the Commission the Governor-General placed strong emphasis on the principles embodied in the Despatch of 1854, and required of it to note how far effect had been given to these principles. Its inquiries were to extend particularly to the questions referred to above, such as primary education, grants-in-aid, self-help and local control, and further facts that might be laid before them by different witnesses.

The Commision met soon after its appointment, spent seven weeks in preliminary investigations and in

* The Missionary members of the Commission were the Rev. Dr. Miller (to be mentioned later) of Madras, the Rev. W. R. Blackett of Calcutta, and the Rev. Dr. Jean of St. Joseph's College, Trichinopoly (Jesuit).

preparing lists of questions to be asked, then eight months in a tour of all the provinces, collecting materials and receiving petitions and hearing witnesses. 193 witnesses were examined, 323 memorials and petitions were received, and so an immense amount of material was collected, which formed the subject of its deliberations for three months more. Its Report covers more than 600 folio pages, and furnishes a careful analysis and scrutiny of nearly every question connected with Indian education up to that time. The conclusions of the Commission are embodied in a list of 222 recommendations, 180 of which were carried unanimously. These form a sort of gist of the Report and deal with the following questions in order. (1) Indigenous Education. (2) Primary Education. (3) Secondary Education. (4) Collegiate Education. (5) Internal Administration of the Educational Department. (6) External Relations of the Department. (7) Classes requiring special treatment, such as Muhammadans, Aboriginal Tribes, Low Castes. (8) Female Education. (9) Legislation. It will be convenient here to consider a few of these questions, such as relate to our subject, and to state the conclusions of the Commission mainly in its own words.

Indigenous Education is education carried on by the natives of India according to their old methods and not conforming to the ordinary rules of the Department of Education. The chief recommendation of the Commission, showing the light in which all such private efforts are to be regarded, is as follows:

> "That all indigenous schools, whether high or low, be recognized and encouraged, if they serve any purpose of secular education whatsoever."

On Primary Education, concerning which there was so much discussion, the Commission emphatically concurred with the views of those who were contending against the state authorities. It stated:

"That while every branch of education can justly claim the fostering care of the state, it is desirable, in the present circumstances of the country, to declare the elementary education of the masses, its provision, extension, and improvement, to be that part of the educational system to which the strenuous efforts of the state should now be directed in a still larger measure than heretofore."

The following resolutions, under Primary Education are of interest to missionary educators, and to certain classes of the people in which missionaries are usually interested:

"That care be taken not to interfere with the freedom of managers of aided schools in the choice of text-books." "That the existing rules as to religious teaching in government schools be applied to all primary schools wholly maintained by Municipal or Local Fund Boards." "That all primary schools wholly maintained at the cost of the school boards, and all primary schools that are aided from the same fund and are not registered as special schools, be understood to be open to all castes and classes of the community."

Under Secondary Education the following and other resolutions did away with certain abuses that had been pointed out:

"That scholarships gained in open competition be tenable, under proper safe-guards, to ensure the progress of the scholarship-holder, at any approved institution for general or special instruction."

In the matter of charging fees some difficulty had arisen, for certain private bodies, in order to attract students, preferred to charge very low fees or none at all; while the educational authorities maintained that all must charge equal fees. The Commission recommended:

"That in order to encourage the establishment of aided schools the managers be not required to charge fees as high as those of a neighboring government school of the same class."

Similar resolutions covered the matter of the last two recommendations under the heading of Collegiate Education. Under the latter head were introduced two recommendations on the much debated question of ethical and religious teaching. They were worded mildly enough to secure the assent of a majority of the members of the Commission, and were meant to secure such provision as was possible for these subjects. They are as follows:

"That an attempt be made to prepare a moral text-book, based upon the fundamental principles of natural religion, such as may be taught in all government and non-government colleges." "That the Principal or one of the professors in each government and aided college deliver to each of the college classes in every session a series of lectures on the duties of a man and a citizen."

In reviewing the Report of the Commission the Governor-General expressed his dissent from these proposals and said:

"It is doubtful whether such a moral text-book as is proposed could be introduced without raising a variety of burning questions; and strongly as it may be urged that a purely secular education is imperfect, it does not appear probable that a text-book of morality, sufficiently vague and colorless to be accepted by Christians, Muhammadans, and Hindus, would do much, especially in the stage of collegiate instruction, to remedy the defects or supply the short-comings of such an education. The same objections appear to apply to the proposal that a series of lectures should be delivered in each college on the duties of a man and of a citizen The Secretary of State intimates his concurrence in the views of the Government of India on this matter, but adds that possibly hereafter some book in the nature of a text-book of Moral Rules may be written of such merit as to render its use desirable. In that event the question can be reconsidered."

The following recommendations of the Commission, on limiting religious instruction according to the wishes of the parents, were likewise rejected by Government:

"That the system of grants-in-aid be based as hitherto, in accordance with paragraph 53 of the Despatch of 1854, on an entire abstinence from interference with the religious instruction conveyed in the institution assisted: provided that when the only institution of any particular grade existing in any town or village is an institution in which religious instruction forms a part of the ordinary course, it shall be open to parents to withdraw their children from attendance at such instruction without forfeiting any of the benefits of the institution." "That a parent be understood to consent to his child's passing through the full curriculum of the school, unless his intention to withdraw him from religious instruction be intimated at the time of the child's first entering the school, or at the beginning of a subsequent term."

On this matter Government said:

"With reference to the modified conscience clause embodied in the proviso to Recommendation 25, the Secretary of State has decided that as no practical difficulty has arisen from the absence of such a condition in the scheme of education laid down in the Despatch, the proviso would better be dropped."

The subject of External Relations of the Department discussed in the eighth chapter of the Report is one of interest to missionary educators. After reviewing the comparative cost of state and aided education, resulting as previously stated, it is recommended as a general principle to be clearly and steadily kept in view:

"That whilst existing state institutions of the higher order should be maintained in complete efficiency wherever they are necessary, the improvement and extension of institutions under private management be the principal care of the Department." "That in ordinary circumstances, the further extension of secondary education in any District be left to the operation of the grant-in-aid system, as soon as that District is provided with an efficient high school, government or other, along with its necessary feeders."

What system is to be adopted to determine the amount of aid to be given by Government? The easiest method is that of payment by results obtained in examinations, where for every scholar who passes an examination a certain definite amount is paid to the manager of the school. Besides making altogether too much of examinations, and favoring various kinds of frauds in connection with the same, this system assumes that schools are already established and have resources of some kind to carry them through preliminary difficulties, so that it gives little encouragement to the setting up of new schools. The following recommendations make clear the Commission's view of the manner in which aid should be given to one department of education (the collegiate):

"That the rate of aid to each college be determined by the strength of the staff, the expenditure on its maintainance, the efficiency of the institution, and the wants of the locality." "That provision be made for special grants to aided colleges, whenever necessary for the supply and renewal of buildings, furniture, libraries, and other apparatus of instruction."

As to conditions of aid the Commission held that the rules should be liberally construed and that everything should be done to further any private effort whatever. The needless delays, both in sanctioning and in paying grants, were severely criticised by the Commission.

The Commission found that there was cause for complaint of want of sympathy on the part of the State towards private effort. A part of the evidence brought before it, stated that "aided schools are looked upon by the educational authorities as excrescences which are to be removed, and the sooner the better." A Director of Public Instruction in Madras "avowed it to be his policy to develop Departmental education *pari passu* with that resulting from private effort." "Scholarships have been confined to Departmental institutions. In one Province scholarships were rigorously withheld from pupils who had received any portion of their education in institutions under private managers." "Rules have been laid down for aided schools which the Department never thought of applying to its own schools." In general, "Only in rare cases has the Department discharged its duty of actively fostering private effort, cold justice is the utmost which as a rule it has been willing to accord."

The various conditions of the success of private effort were now clearly outlined. In addition to what has already been stated as the chief principles, "first of all necessary to be understood," the following were deemed of considerable weight:

"That those who assist the State by managing them (schools) should have great influence in determining all questions of general educational policy......In determining all such matters as the arrangement or conduct of public examinations, the rate of fees, the terms of admission, the course of study, or the forms of periodical returns......the Director of Public Instruction should be guided as much by the views of those interested in aided education as by those of Departmental officers." "Freedom be not interfered with......It equally forbids all endeavors to impose a rigid routine of study or a particular set of text-books upon all schools......In short, the Department should let aided institutions grow after their own fashion, interfering with that growth only in cases of extreme necessity." "Wherever it (private effort) becomes fit to do the work needed, the Department should remove its own institutions, as the Despatch of 1854 contemplates." "Private effort is the one that should increase, and the direct agency of the Department is the one that should diminish."

The question of the gradual withdrawal of the State from direct participation in the work of education and handing the same over to private bodies is discussed at full length in the Report. The chief arguments in favor of such withdrawal are first, that of economy, which bulks the largest, then that of securing variety of effort, and lastly that it gives encouragement to religious instruction. The arguments opposed to withdrawal are the danger of a false impression being made on the people that Government has lost interest in education, and the difficulty of maintaining especially higher education by native effort. The bearing of the policy of withdrawal on Missionary Education is fully discussed and deserves quoting in part :—

"The question how far the withdrawal of the State from the direct provision of means for higher education would throw such education into the hands of missionary bodies, held the foremost place in all the evidence bearing on the topic of withdrawal. Prominent officers of the Department and many native gentlemen argued strongly against any withdrawal, on the ground that it must practically hand over higher education to missionaries. As a rule, the missionary witnesses themselves, while generally advocating the policy of withdrawal, expressed quite the contrary opinion, stating that they neither expected nor desired that any power over education given up by the Department should pass into their hands. In a country with such varied needs as India, we should deprecate any measure which would throw excessive influence over higher education into the hands of any single agency which, however benevolent and earnest, cannot on all points be in sympathy with the mass of the community."

"At the same time we think it well to put on record our unanimous opinion that withdrawal of direct departmental agency should not take place in favor of missionary bodies, and that departmental institutions of the higher order should not be transferred to missionary management."

"In the point of view in which we are at present considering the question, missionary institutions hold an intermediate position between those managed by the Department and those managed by the people for themselves. On the one hand, they are the outcome of private effort, but on the other they are not strictly local; nor will encouragement to them directly foster those habits of self-reliance and combination for purposes of public utility, which it is one of the objects of the grant-in-aid system to develop.........It must not be forgotten that the private effort which it is mainly intended to evoke is that of the people themselves. Natives of India must constitute the most important of all agencies if educational means are ever to be co-extensive with educational wants. Other agencies may hold a prominent place for a time, and may always find some place in a system in which great variety is on every ground desirable. But the higher education of the country will not be on a basis that can be regarded as permanent or safe, nor will it receive the wide extension that is needed, until the larger part of it at all events is provided and managed by the people of the country for themselves."

The subject of Female Education received careful attention on the part of the Commission and everything possible was done to stimulate this very needy branch of Indian education. Every encouragement is to be given to it and grants are to be liberal and easily obtained. The following are a few of the more important recommendations :—

"That all female schools or orphanages, whether on a religious basis or not, be eligible for aid so far as they produce any secular results, such as a knowledge of reading or of writing." "That the conditions of aid to girls' schools be easier than to boys' schools, and the rates higher—more especially in the case of those established for poor or for low caste girls." "That the rules for grants be so framed as to allow for the fact that girls' schools generally contain a large proportion of beginners, and of those who cannot attend school for so many hours a day, or with such regularity, as boys." "That the standards of instruction for primary girls' schools be simpler than those for boys' schools, and be drawn up with special reference to the requirements of home life, and to the occupations open to women,"

Some of the most important of the Commission's recommendations refer to the increase of public funds required for aided education :

"It seems inevitable that our recommendations must lead to increased expenditure in two directions. In Chapter VIII we have recommended that a periodically increasing provision be made in the educational budget of each Province for the expansion of aided institutions."

The need of education is emphasized by the figures given in the Report, which show that in the territory under British rule, containing 859,844 square miles with 552,379 villages and towns, inhabited by 202,604,080 persons, there were only 112,218 schools, and 2,643,978 Indian children or adults at school in 1881-82. The proportion of pupils to the children of school going age is given for all India to be 16 per cent for males and less than 1 per cent for females; while in one whole province it is as low as 8 per cent for males and .28 per cent for females. Out of a hundred and three millions of males about ninety-three and a quarter millions were wholly illiterate; and of the female population, numbering 99,700,000 no less than 99,500,000 are returned in the census as unable to read or write.

There is no doubt that the work of the Education Commission was a decided success and that it gave a great impulse to education, and particularly to private efforts. As far as the Report could help it, missionary education was favored as much as the subject needed or deserved, and in accordance with the firm principle of neutrality no note was taken of the missionary or evangelistic side of this work, but it was regarded as one of the forms of private effort, to be welcomed and encouraged as one of the legitimate ways in which India is to be educated. In one part alone does it seem that missionary education was discriminated against, in the matter of transference of government institutions to private bodies, where it was expressly recommended that they be not transferred to missionary societies but to local native bodies. The reasons given are good, and it is clear that the objection is not to missionaries as such, but to the fact that they are foreigners, and that every effort must be made to stimulate and encourage the people to help themselves. Where the Indian Christian community is strong enough Government will favor it as much as any private body. Sufficient has been quoted and explained to show the relation which from that time on is considered normal between the Government and aided education, and also the large place which the latter holds in the system of education in India. The Report of the Commission as a whole was approved by the Government of India, with the exceptions already noted, by its action of the 23rd October, 1884, and remains till to-day a part of the educational law of the land.

In the next chapter, the History of Missionary Education will be brought up to the present date, and the influence of the legislation of 1882-84 will be manifest.

CHAPTER IV.

MODERN MISSIONARY EDUCATION, 1882-1907.

How did the missionaries look upon the Commission of 1882 and its Report ? Their answer can best be seen in the manner in which they have carried on their work since that time. There is no doubt that the Commission's work, which recognized their position, had a share in the impulses given which caused the increase both in numbers and efficiency of their work during this period. But there were other causes. In the first place, greater attention has been paid to the subject of education in the home countries, both in the United States and in Great Britain. Then also, although there were giants in intellect as well as in spiritual power among the missionaries of former days, yet the standard of the educational qualifications of the whole class of missionaries has doubtless been raised of recent years. Again, there has been a great increase all along the line of missionary effort, in evangelism, medical work, and other forms of Christian and philanthropic effort, as well as in education ; and all this work has become much better organized than was possible before. But perhaps above all, it has become more and more manifest that if Christianity is to make any real impression upon India, if India is ever to be Christianized, the fountain head of its life must be assailed. This question will be more fully discussed under the Theory of Missionary Education.

In previous chapters it was easy to point to a few

men who were prominent in this work. In the period since 1882 so many have come and joined in this great movement that it is almost impossible to select the best representatives. Many who began their career before 1882 have continued up to the present time. Foremost among these is to be mentioned the Honorable the Rev. William Miller, M.A., LL.D., D.D., C.I.E., who came to India in 1863, and has for forty-three years occupied the high position of Principal of the Madras Christian College. A member of the Education Commission of 1882, he was also one of the chief witnesses that were called to testify before the Universities' Commission of 1902. He is one of the oldest Fellows of the Madras University, and was elected its vice-chancellor in 1901. He was four times appointed by the Government of Madras as the University member of the Legislative Council. His name is especially familiar to readers of Missionary Conference Reports, for in most of these he took a very important part advocating the cause of Christian education for India in the strongest terms and on the broadest basis. He prepared one of the principal papers at each of the following Conferences of Missions :—Allahabad, 1872; Bangalore, 1879; Calcutta, 1882; London, 1888; Chicago, 1893; Madras, 1900. He has been noted especially for his advocacy of higher Christian education, not on the grounds of its furnishing a means of direct conversion, nor even of its presenting opportunities of proclaiming the gospel to certain classes, but rather as a preparatory agency, to make educated India ready to receive the gospel. But his greatest work has been in connection with the college where he labored so long as Principal and Professor of the English Language and Literature. He gave himself heart and soul and fortune for the good of the college, and some of its beautiful buildings put up in recent years were largely the gifts of himself and members of his family. He was a teacher of marked ability, and won the universal admiration and esteem of his students. The graduates and other late students of this institution a few years ago paid a glowing tribute of their affection and esteem for Dr. Miller by raising a subscription and putting up a large bronze statue, representing his figure, in a public highway of Madras opposite the college. He is the only missionary in India who has been so honored. The Government of India has also awarded him the noted Kaiser-i-Hind Gold Medal, at a recent celebration of the King's birthday, in recognition of his distinguished services in the cause of Indian education.

Other faithful and noted laborers during this period were the Rev. D. Mackichan, M.A., D.D., LL.D., principal since 1884 of the Wilson College at Bombay, the only missionary among the seven members of the Universities' Commission of 1902, and Vice-chancellor of the Bombay University: and also the Rev. J. C. R. Ewing, M.A., D.D., Ph.D., principal of the Forman Christian College, Lahore, "than whom there is no man in the Province better known and more highly esteemed and more greatly loved by all classes of the people, not excepting the Lieutenant-Governor of the Punjab." * Dr. Ewing also was awarded last year the Kaiser-i-Hind Gold Medal in honor of his services. But where there are so many noted names it is hard to select a few for particular record. Out of a total of 156 witnesses who were asked to give their advice and counsel to the Universities' Commission in 1902, there were twenty-five missionary educators, and all of them were men of experience and

* The testimony of a Brahman student of Lahore.

of choice talent in this field of work, capable of taking a high place anywhere, and exercising a remarkable influence over the whole system of education in India.

In order to gain some idea of the present condition of missionary education in India we shall make a brief survey of the work of the various societies based largely on their Reports for 1905-06. The American Congregationalists have three missions in India, located in the Maratha country, in Madura, and in the island of Ceylon. One of their most interesting schools is one for blind children in Bombay, containing fifty pupils, who are taught not only the ordinary elementary branches but also various industries. Some are taught type-writing and some are given music lessons on the piano. The school receives no money from the regular Board, but is supported by voluntary gifts, which seem to have come in very liberally. The Society's college in Madura is growing in importance, was recently highly commended by the Governor of Madras, and is enlisting the sympathy of people with money, as seen in the recent gift of $23,000, for improved buildings and apparatus. In Jaffna they have a college, teaching to the Bachelor's degree, with 105 students in the college department, and four missionary instructors.

The American Baptists have missions in Burma and in the Telugu country, with a second grade college in each field. The principal of the Rangoon Baptist College reports a successful year and indicates enlargements and advancement that are contemplated. Raising the grade of the College from First Arts to Bachelor of Arts, and providing additional buildings for the college, are among his plans, which have also met the approval of the Board at home. The Lieutenant-Governor of Burma presided at the Annual Prize Giving and said among other things: "I congratulate the principal, professors and teachers on the progress that has been made. I have expressed elsewhere my hope that before long the projected erection of this institution to a college of the first grade will be accomplished. As far as possible Government will assist and encourage the aspirations of your Reverend principal and his assistants to bring this college to a foremost place among the educational institutions of the province."

The American Presbyterians have three colleges, one in Lahore, one in Allahabad, and one in Mussoorie for American and English pupils. Among Presbyterian institutions must also be reckoned the Canadian Mission College at Indore, Central Provinces; and the Voorhees College at Vellore, maintained by the Reformed Church in America; and the Gordon Mission College, at Rawalpindi, maintained by the United Presbyterians. The Forman Christian College at Lahore is the largest Christian college outside of the three Presidency towns, having over 400 students in the college department. It wields a tremendous influence over the whole Punjab. Dr. Ewing, the principal, writes: "It is the constant effort of the professors to come into personal contact with the men. One period of each day is devoted to teaching the Word of God. The opportunity furnished by the college for representing to the educated classes of the Province the spirit and teachings of Christ is unique. The men come to us from all quarters of the Punjab and return after years of life spent under these influences, to carry with them many of those ideas which are working mighty changes in the thought of the entire people. The prosperity and popularity of the college has been and is great."

The Lutherans have one of the largest and most successful missions in South India. At the head of a well organized system of education is the Watts' Memorial College at Guntur, and the principal speaks of the embarrassment of growing popularity: "The college needs not luxuries but merely room to receive those who are willing to come and put themselves under the influence of a Christian instruction. When the Watts' Memorial building was erected the most sanguine could not have hoped that in ten years it would be outgrown."

The Methodists have two flourishing institutions at Lucknow, the Reid Christian College for men, and the Isabella Thoburn College for women, the only Woman's college in India established by American missionaries. The principal of the former institution reports that last year was the best in their history, as seen both in high intellectual results and in marked spiritual results as well. "Scores of students have been converted and quickened to new life. Nineteen young men have consecrated their lives to the ministry."

Nearly three-fourths of the Christian colleges of India are maintained by British societies, and of these more than half, or nineteen in number, are supported by the Church of England societies, including the Society for the Propagation of the Gospel. The oldest and most prominent of the Church Missionary Society's colleges is St. John's College at Agra, which has 175 students in the college department. Regarding this school their latest Report says: "In more recent years owing to the rapid increase of the Indian Christian community, the object of the institution has become somewhat changed. While welcoming as before all Hindus and Muhammadans, desirous of receiving a liberal education under Christian influences, the College has become recognized as an institution where the education of Indian Christian youths is also made a matter of primary importance." This society has the unique distinction of maintaining the only remaining Woman's college in India, at Palamcotta. The S.P.G. have large and important institutions at Trichinopoly and at Delhi. In their work they have a very able staff of missionary instructors, and a consequently high grade of teaching is maintained both in secular and religious matters. The problem of the college as an evangelistic agency is dealt with in several of the reports in a suggestive manner. The following extracts may be quoted: "We have no actual conversions to report, but there are many evident signs that the daily system of religious instruction, given throughout the school, is not without its fruit." "We are not, however, single in the fewness of our converts: nowhere in India is any great number being gathered into the church from the class with which we have to deal, the educated class." "The life of Christ was held up as the one perfect standard for those who aspired to the highest and best life possible to human beings, his redemption as the one perfect sacrifice for human sin, and his risen life as the one perfect source of spiritual power." "All the age-long experience, which has nursed and tended and moulded the making of Indian manhood, resists the missionary's appeal; and against such tremendous influence mere argument is powerless... . The missionary ought to feel no discouragement on finding out that convictions such as these do not vanish before a syllogism. If he is wise he will recognize that such convictions must be slow in their decay, and that new convictions, if they are to be based deep enough to found a religion upon, must in like manner be of very slow formation. And when we note the countless Christian influences which now play upon the educated people of India, we may well be content to await patiently the time when these slow but sure influences will mould the convictions into a Christian form."

The Wesleyan Missionary Society maintains six colleges in India and Ceylon, all of the second grade. The London Missionary Society maintains four colleges, one of the first grade, with nearly a hundred students in the college department, at Bhowanipore, near Calcutta. They speak of the gradual modification of their aims in this their principal institution: "The original aim of our institution was evangelistic, to win Hindus for Christ by means of a sound Christian education. As the Christian community of Bhowanipore gradually attained importance our institution came to be of considerable value also as a training school for young Christians. Yet this long remained subordinate to the primary aim. It is now, however, becoming daily more possible to evangelize the educated young men of Calcutta by other and simpler means than the educational method—by preaching, personal intercourse, the press, etc., while the necessity for providing as thoroughly as possible for the higher education of the Christian community daily asserts itself more clearly."

We have reserved to the last the record of Scotland's great institutions, about which a whole book could be written. With 6000 students in seven institutions, of whom 2400 are in the college department, taught by twenty-four able Scotch teachers, graduates of Edinburgh, Glasgow, Oxford, and Cambridge, besides a large Indian staff; the amount of good thus contributed by Scotland as a free gift to educated India is incalculable. Nearly one-half the total number of college students of the Christian colleges of India are enrolled in Scottish colleges; while all the American societies together, though having just double the number of colleges, have only one-third as many students as there are in the Scottish institutions. First of all there is the original college founded by Dr. Duff in 1830, split up into two on account of the disruption in the home churches in 1843, and meeting then with various vicissitudes; but now for a period of more than forty years two strong colleges have been maintained in Calcutta by these two churches. But arrangements have just happily been completed this year, whereby the two colleges will be re-united, and so form the largest Christian college in India, wherein, if the numbers remain, there will be a thousand college students and nearly the same number in the high school. Special preparations are being made for a strong aggressive Christian propaganda in this the capital city of the Indian Empire. At least one of the ordained staff will give all his strength to evangelistic work among the students, besides that carried on daily in the classes, visiting the hostels and the homes of local students, and preaching in the public squares.

The second to be founded by the Scottish Church is the Wilson College at Bombay, named after its founder, the Rev. John Wilson. In 1843, in Bombay as in Calcutta, the disruption led to the opening of a second college, which later became a high school. In 1889, with funds raised by Dr. Mackichan in Scotland and in India, and with generous grants from the Bombay government, the fine academic structure at the head of Black Bay was opened. It is the largest college in Western India, and has been the means of obtaining some of the strongest converts in India from all classes of the Indian nation, Hindus, Muhammadans, and Parsees. The many lady students and graduates from this college form a remarkable feature of its classes.

The Madras Christian College was founded in 1837 by the Rev. John Anderson, and was developed by Dr. William Miller and his many colleagues into the largest and best equipped college in the East. In the number of Indian Christians among its students, in the character and influence of the men whom it sends forth every year to fill high places in the South of India and in the Feudatory States, and in its influence in elevating public life and opinion, this institution is remarkable. In 1905 it reported 900 students in the high school and 800 in the college department. Of the total number of graduates of the 15 colleges connected with the Madras University nearly one-third are graduates from this college. But its chief feature is that it is a union college. In 1877 Dr. Miller's far-seeing scheme came into effect, by which the Scottish Church and the Church Missionary and Wesleyan Societies together contribute $10,000 a year; the College Council consists of representatives of all the evangelical and Anglican missions of South India.

The recent reports of all these colleges speak of the dearth in spiritual results, such as can be tabulated. After reviewing the Bible teaching done by Scottish missionary teachers on the basis of the Gospels and the Acts, which was received with great attention by the students, the report says: "It is difficult to explain why more college men do not profess to be Christians. The probable answer is to be found in family considerations, but the main influences which retard the progress of Christianity are (1) the materialistic tendency of Western thinking and the prevalence of agnosticism in the world at large and (2) the growing spirit of nationality. There is more of an anti-Christian feeling in the air than there has been in the last fifteen years and this feeling is not based on religious principles but on nationalism and loyalty to Hindu practice." "To us who enjoy the unique opportunity which a Christian college provides for coming into contact with these classes, it is a continual joy to give the message of the gospel of the grace of God to increasing numbers of the young minds of India. We rejoice in the widening field of Christian influence that is being opened up for the church of Christ in India, we pray to be made more faithful in the use of our opportunities, and leave to him who giveth the increase the result of all our sowing and our watering the Word."

Reference has been made to the Universities Commission of 1902. Just as the first period ended with the Parliamentary investigations and legislation culminating in Bentinck's proclamation of 1835; and the second period ended in the great Despatch of 1854, called the Magna Charta of Indian education; and the third period saw at its close the Education Commission's Report of 1882; so the fourth period, covering as the others approximately twenty-five years, culminated in the appointment of the Universities Commission, to investigate the affairs of the Universities and of education generally throughout India. The first three of these legislative measures were profoundly influenced by missionaries. Bentinck's proclamation, based on Macauley's minute, was framed entirely on the model furnished by Alexander Duff in his English school. The Despatch of the Court of Directors of 1854 was to a large extent a verbatim copy of a plan outlined by Duff in his testimony before the committee appointed by Parliament. The investigations of 1882 were undertaken almost entirely at the instigation of missionary educators, who complained of grievances and discriminations that were being made against them and their work. But it was not so with the legislation of 1902-1904. By this time the British

Government, the native community, and the missionaries had come to more of a mutual understanding of their different positions as regards the educational problems of India, and the part that each is to play in working them out. And though the aims of these three are not identical, yet it is safe to say that there is now more complete harmony in the practical details of their work than there has ever been before.

The present era of reform was inaugurated by Lord Curzon, Viceroy of India, 1899-1905, who in September, 1901, called together the Directors of Public Instruction of every province in India and also representatives of the principal colleges throughout India to a meeting in Simla, for the purpose of consulting with them about the state and the needs of all branches of education.* Four departments of education were considered: University Education, Secondary Education, Primary Education, and Technical Education. Curzon expressed himself amazed at the amount that was still left undone after seventy years of effort on the part of the Government on behalf of education in India. With four and a half millions of pupils in school, children and adults, out of a population of three hundred millions, provision was made for the education of only one in five boys and for only one in forty girls; and for this the contribution of the State amounted to but little over one million sterling. The following striking sentences from his opening address illustrate his thoughts. "The question of education concerns not only the Viceroy and his Council and the educational officers, but all the educated persons and the millions of uneducated as well." "The responsibility of the Imperial Government I avow. I hold the

* See "Curzon in India," pp. 313-339.

education of the Indian people to be as much a duty of the central Government as the police of our cities and the taxation of our citizens." "One of the first claims upon its bounty that Government would do well to acknowledge will be the education of the masses" "The most conspicuous blot on the educational system of India is the state of female education." "Religious instruction is impossible in government schools, yet moral teaching must rest on a religious foundation. All that the Government can insist on at the present time is good teachers, good text-books, good boarding-houses for the students, and so in an indirect way provide for the building up of good character."

It may be well to quote in this connection an extract from the Government of India's Resolution on Education in India, following the Report of the Universities Commission, dated 11th March, 1904, on the subject, "Ethics of Education."

"The remark has often been made that the extension in India of an education modelled upon European principles and so far as government institutions are concerned, purely secular in its character, has stimulated tendencies unfavorable to discipline and has encouraged the growth of a spirit of irreverence in the rising generation. If any schools or colleges produce this result they fail to realize the object with which they are established—of promoting the moral no less than the intellectual and physical well-being of their students. It is the settled policy of Government to abstain from interfering with the religious instruction given in aided schools. Many of these, maintained by native managers or by missionary bodies in various parts of the Empire, supply religious and ethical instruction to complete the educational training of their scholars. In government institutions the instruction is, and must continue to be, exclusively secular. In such cases the remedy for the evil tendency noticed above is to be sought, not so much in any formal methods of teaching conduct by means of moral text-books or primers of personal ethics, as in the influence of carefully selected and trained teachers, the maintenance of a high standard of discipline, the institution of well-managed hostels, the proper selection of text-books such as biographies, which teach by example, and above all in the association of teachers and pupils in the common interests of their daily life."

We note in the above official statement, as in many like opinions expressed by high authorities in the British administration, the evidently implied approval of the religious instruction given in aided schools.

The course of the reforms begun in 1901 and continuing till the present time does not specifically affect mission institutions. Missionaries are taking a large share in the discussions and are intensely interested in many of the problems to be solved, but mainly because they are interested in a general way in the education of the multitudes of India. They stand perhaps nearer to the masses in India and sympathise more deeply with them and understand them better and are more trusted by them than any others that concern themselves on their behalf in the educational department of the State, whether European or high caste Indian.

One way in which recent legislation is affecting mission institutions along with others is the insistence by Government on a higher grade of teaching, especially in science, and on the provision of better apparatus for the same. Many mission schools are driven hard to find the necessary means for the improved equipment required, and the question is being asked anew by some: "Does it pay to spend so much mission money on secular teaching of non-Christians"? The further insistence by Government that all second grade colleges, teaching to the end of the sophomore year, shall rise to a higher standard and shall be prepared to teach the Arts course to the Bachelor's degree, or else shall be disaffiliated and reduced to high schools, will seriously affect many mission institutions. There are forty second grade mission colleges in India, twenty-two of which are connected with the Madras University. They are doing a useful service and are educating many young men and young women, especially of the Christian community, up to as high a standard as is demanded by present circumstances. Many of these institutions must choose between making no provision for the higher education, such as it is, of the Christian young people around them, or else at a heavy expense provide a still higher education where it is not demanded, resulting at best in a poor equipment and diminutive classes in the last two years of the college course. On the other hand, the demands for a complete college course are increasing year by year, and are almost as much felt now as demands for a second grade education were at the time that many of these colleges were founded: and a number of these institutions were already contemplating the step of raising their grade quite apart from the action of Government. All these schools are carefully considering whether it will be wiser to recede or to advance: there will be cases, perhaps not few, where the educational needs, both of the Christian community and of the general community surrounding the college, can be adequately met by maintaining a well-equipped mission high school, especially where there are other colleges near at hand. There will be others who plainly see the need of advancing now to a higher standard and a higher and larger influence among all classes of the community. *

* For the present the measure above referred to will not be insisted on by the Government.

Apart from this special question there are larger problems now being dealt with by the Educational Department of the State, and it would seem that the whole question of aided education, and of the part that missionaries are to perform in the matter, is once more to be up for discussion. This is particularly the case in the Madras Presidency, where the Government has just issued a new set of Educational Rules and a new Grant-in-aid Code which seriously affect the relations of aided education to the general scheme, especially in the matter of primary education, and to a large extent of secondary education as well. The present tendency of the Department of Education appears to be distinctly away from the policy of the Despatch of 1854, which was re-affirmed in 1882-84, and is in the direction of a system of government schools, wholly controlled by the Department. Grants to aided education will be materially reduced, and the conditions of earning them will be harder to meet, while Government reserves to itself a greater amount of control in the internal operations of aided schools. The fear is expressed by some recent writers on the subject that the present policy of Government marks the beginning of the end of aided education. Others speak more hopefully of the situation and interpret the action of Government as due to its having awakened to the real necessities of the case and to its desire to really provide for the education of the masses of the people. There is no doubt that Government will in due time give its own interpretation, but matters are not yet well enough determined for us to be able to pass judgment upon them; but it is likely to prove an interesting and important question, which will have an important bearing on the future of missionary education in India. * There is not the least danger that the outcome will be disastrous, or that missionaries will think of abandoning this work. Educational missions have a deeper foundation than government support, being based upon the need there is for just this kind of effort in conjunction with the whole campaign for the Christian conquest of India.

In conclusion, we shall consider a few figures and call attention to the statistical tables, which for convenience are placed at the end of this book. These will make evident the strength and the conditions of missionary education as accurately as possible at the present time.†

The growth of missionary education during this period has more than kept up with the pace of former times. The total number of schools has increased from 5,627 to 11,813. The number of pupils and students in all mission schools has increased since 1882 from 241,646 to 527,660, in which number Zenana pupils also are included. Of this number about 5,300 are in the college departments of the various colleges. This figure has often

---

* References :—Martin : A Survey of our Educational Work in the Light of Present Conditions ; *Baptist Missionary Review*, Ongole, India, July, 1906. Lucas : The Educational Policy as indicated in The New Code ; *The Harvest Field*, Mysore, India, September, 1906. Pollard : The Government Educational Policy in Relation to Missionary Societies ; *Idem*, November, 1906.

† It has been impossible to obtain all the figures desired. Some societies do not publish such statistics in their reports, and some publish no reports at all. A few have not responded to our inquiries. The figures given are based on the latest reports of the societies, on the Government Census for 1901, on the Government Quinquennial Review for 1887-1902, and on the Statistical Tables of Protestant Missions, published by the Baptist Mission Press, Calcutta, in 1882, 1892, 1902. A few are borrowed from Bishop Thoburn's Christian Conquest of India. Our figures include those for Burma and Ceylon.

been given larger, owing to the fact that scholars in some high schools connected with colleges have been counted as college students.

The list of colleges in the first table is as far as we know the most complete list of the kind ever compiled. Of the fifty-two Protestant colleges now in existence thirty-three were raised to this grade and affiliated to the universities after 1882, showing the great activity in this branch of work in recent years. These colleges are fairly well distributed over the whole land and are placing the people from nearly all parts within reach of Christian education. Still, there are at least fifteen large cities in India, with over 100,000 population each, that have no Protestant Christian college. Besides these there are more than forty towns, with a population of more than 50,000 each, without Christian colleges.

In the second table of statistics we have given detailed figures of eight American societies and of six British societies, selecting only those that have college work in India, and lumping the others together. We are thus enabled to compare what share the different nations have in this work. In columns 6 and 7 we see the comparative strength of the preaching and teaching forces, and in columns 8 and 9 we see the number of churches or meeting places compared with the number of schools, while in columns 10 and 13 we may compare the total number of scholars in all schools with the communicant members of the churches. We see that in the grand totals the proportion of Indian preachers to teachers is approximately as 20 to 23; that of churches to schools as 20 to 24; and that of communicant members to school pupils as 20 to 22; giving throughout a small balance in favor of the educational work as distinguished from the ecclesiastical.

In a separate table the growth of missionary education since 1830 is given by decades, which shows a steady growth under each item. The number of colleges and the number of high schools are given according to the universities with which they are affiliated. The latter figures are probably less than the actual, it having been impossible to obtain exact statistics. The number is less than that usually given as that of mission high schools or secondary schools in India, as it includes only those that prepare students for the matriculation examinations of the various universities.

One of the most encouraging facts that a study of the Indian Census tables brings to our notice is the advance that the Christian population has made over the rest of the people. In considering a few figures which we are about to quote, two things must be borne in mind: first, that the Christian community has come largely from the lowest class of the people, and second, that while the statistics and averages are given for the whole Christian community, yet the educational condition of the Protestants is very much better than that of the Roman Catholic and Syrian Christians, who form more than two-thirds of the whole Christian population. Remembering these facts let us note among the different religions; first, what proportion of children are in school, and second, what proportion of the people can read and write.

The number of the children of school-going age, in all schools:

	Hindus	Muhammadans	Buddhists	Christians
Boys	1 in 5	1 in 6	1 in 5	1 in 2
Girls	1 in 51	1 in 81	1 in 21	1 in 2

The number of girls of school-going age, who are in secondary schools:—

Hindus	Muhammadans	Christians
1 in 3703;	1 in 20,000;	1 in 55.

Of a total of 393,163 girls in all schools, 45,844 are Indian Christians, which is nearly 12 per cent.; while Christians form only one per cent. of the population.

Here are the numbers of the population, according to religions, who can read and write:—

	Hindus	Muhammadans	Buddhists	Christians
Males	1 in 10½	1 in 16½	1 in 2½	1 in 3½
Females	1 in 213	1 in 328	1 in 24	1 in 8

These figures, and many more that could be given, are eloquent proofs of the progress that the Christian community is making in India.

It has been difficult to estimate the number of missionaries whose time is wholly devoted to educational work, but it is safe to assume that the same proportion of effort on their part is devoted to educational work, as we saw in the case of Indian workers. (p. 90) This would mean that of the 4,400 missionaries about 2,350 must be credited to the educational work, not as showing the number who are devoted to this exclusively, but indicating, if a separation could be made in their duties, the amount of time and effort all the missionaries of India give to school work of various sorts. We are certain that this number so credited to educational effort is somewhat less than the actual. Similarly, with regard to the expense of missionary education in India, it has been impossible to obtain even approximate figures. As the latest Government Quinquennial Report says: "Unfortunately there are in most provinces no available statistics regarding mission institutions and their pupils, and it is not therefore possible to give an accurate account of the work of the mission societies." But fortunately the figures are given for one province in the Report of the Director of Public Instruction for the Madras Presidency, which contains the following :—" From a special return furnished by the heads of missionary bodies, it appears that missions administered an expenditure of 22.9 lakhs of rupees on directly educational purposes. Of this amount 9.8 lakhs were provided from mission funds, 5.7 lakhs from grants-in-aid, .3 lakhs from endowments, etc., and 7.1 from fees."* Taking the amount provided by mission funds, and bearing in mind that this in most cases does not include any account of the foreign missionaries' salaries, we see that it costs the missionaries $326,666 (at three rupees to the dollar) to educate about 200,300 pupils of all kinds, (this being the number of pupils in mission schools in the Madras Presidency) giving an average expenditure on each pupil per year of $1.63. At this rate Protestant missions spend $860,085.80 annually on 527,660 pupils in all India ; but we have not counted the cost of the missionaries' salaries. Taking, then, the salaries of 2350 missionaries (above estimated), at $500 per year, we have $1,175,000, and adding to the previous figures we obtain $2,035,085 as the total direct expenditure by Protestant missionaries on education in India.

Now, taking another mode of calculation, and assuming that one-half of the total mission expenditure goes for educational work, inclusive of the salaries of missionaries, according to their time employed in this

---

* Report, 1904-1905, p 8.

work,* and taking as a basis the expenditure reported by the ten largest societies, and the number of pupils in their schools, we obtain an average expenditure of nearly $4.00 for each pupil per year. Multiplying this by the total number of pupils, we obtain $2,110,640 which is very nearly the same as the other figure. But the amount administered by missionaries on the education of India is something larger than the amount provided from mission funds, as seen from the quotation of the Director's Report above. Here the ratio of the amount provided from mission funds to the total amount administered by them was found to be as 9.8 to 22.9. With this as a basis, and not mixing up the missionaries' salaries in the proportion, the amount adminstered by missionaries, exclusive of their own salaries, appears to be $2,009,792. Adding again their own salaries we have $3,184,792.

The following figures are repeated here for easy reference :—

Total amount provided from mission funds for the education of India each year, including the cost of missionary supervision :	$2,000,000
Total amount administered by missionaries each year, ...	$3,185,000
Total number of teachers, Indian and foreign ...	22,270
Total number of mission schools	11,813
Total number taught in mission schools	527,660
Total number of mission high schools	192
Number of mission colleges	52
Students in mission colleges, ...	5,300

* This estimate is based on the proportion of Indian teachers and preachers, schools and churches, etc., above noticed; but the same ratio is assumed by Prof. L. E. Martin, in the *Baptist Missionary Review*, July, 1906, p. 274, who says: "It is safe to say that nearly one-half of the total amount of the appropriation for the whole mission goes for education."

The following figures compare the number of Protestant mission schools, students, expenses, etc., with the totals for all India, or otherwise, as indicated, including government and private effort :—

	Total	Mission	Per cent mission.
No. of arts colleges, Madras Pres'y	40	16	40
Students in college dep't, do.	4,539	1,696	37
High schools, ... do.	197	77	39
Students in high school dep't, do.	21,540	6,832	32
Girls' high schools, do.	26	9	34
High school students, girls, do.	562	276	49
Public schools, all kinds, do.	*22,012	* 4,706	21
Pupils in all schools, do.	841,034	* 200,299	23
Public schools of all kinds in all India	103,347	11,813	11
Total number taught in all India	4,521,000	527,660	12
Total expense, (approximate)	$13,000,000	$3,185,000	24
Students in college dep't, all India	17,651	5,300	30

* These figures include Roman Catholic institutions and pupils.

PART I.

THE THEORY OF MISSIONARY EDUCATION.

CHAPTER I.

THE AIM OF MISSIONARY EDUCATION.

Having thus far traced the history of missionary education in India, and presented some of the external conditions of the work, attention will be devoted in the remainder of this book to an inner view of the situation, and several important questions will be considered that have to do with the successful carrying out of the undertaking. What is a Christian college in India and what does it aim to do? And what is the whole scheme of Missionary Education and what is its purpose? It should be noted at the outset that missionary educational agencies in India aim at two distinct sets of objects, as they deal with either the Christian or the non-Christian community. About the former, which admits of little doubt or discussion, much need not be said. The aim of Christian education as it affects the Christian community is first, spiritual, for the purpose of training it in Christian doctrine; second, secular, for the purpose of training the intellect and developing the whole character and all the powers of, at least, the rising generation of Christians, so that they may become fit to hold a high position and exert a powerful influence on their surroundings. The training of Christian workers, both teachers and preachers, is a part of this work, and forms probably the most important part of the whole campaign planned by foreign missionaries for the evangelisation of India. Every missionary society, even from the earliest times, has tried to do something for the education of the children of converts and for the training of Christian workers. With the present extensive operations of missionary societies in India, and the large number of adherents scattered about among many thousands of villages, it is a great undertaking to provide even a little elementary school in every village where there are a few Christians, and this alone has occupied much of the time of nearly all missionaries. Some missionaries have as many as 150 schools scattered over many miles of territory, of which they are in reality inspectors and superintendents. In each of these there is a teacher, who acts also as pastor over the small flock of Christians. Usually boys and girls, Christian and non-Christian, come to this school, which is often the only means of education in the village. Their education consists of reading, writing, arithmetic, geography, and a few facts of hygiene, botany, and natural history: but great emphasis is laid on the teaching of Bible stories and Christian hymns, and perhaps a catechism. In many of the larger villages missionaries have established schools for high-caste children of non-Christians. The course of instruction is the same, though usually a little more efficiently carried out. In towns where missionaries reside many high schools have been established, a few of them primarily for Christian pupils, but the majority of them having the larger number of their pupils from non-Christian homes. These teach the full high-school course up to the university entrance examination. The course consists of (1) English Language, first, hardest, and most important; (2) a Second Language, which may be Latin, Greek, Hebrew, French, German, or any Indian language, either classical or vernacular; (3) Mathematics, consisting of Arithmetic, Algebra, and Geometry; and (4) Elementary Physical Science, Chemistry, History and Geography of India and of England. In addition to this is a thorough and systematic course in the Bible, Old and New Testaments, to which about one-sixth of the time of the school is usually given.

At the top of the missionary education scheme is the Christian college, of which there are about seventy in India, teaching the regular Literary or Arts course up to the end of the Sophomore year, as in the Second Grade colleges, or to the Bachelor's or Master's or Doctor's degrees. The plan of a Christian college in India is not very different from that of a Christian or denominational college in America, except that a great deal more is made of Scripture lessons. The same careful attention is paid to Bible study as in the case of the high schools, usually the foreign missionary himself giving a large share of his time to instruction in religious knowledge. More than forty per cent. of the colleges of India are under missionary management, so that missionaries control a considerable portion of the higher education of the country, and it is well to ask what are the distinct aims of this higher education.

It is not easy here always to distinguish the two objects above referred to, namely, that of strengthening and training the Christian community, and that of training and educating non-Christians; for the two are often combined and nearly all mission high schools and colleges are open to all classes of the people. Some missionaries, indeed, find their excuse for having a college at all in the need there is for the higher training of Christian youths, believing that it is easy and inexpensive to admit others in addition to these, and seeing, moreover, what is now without question, that the influence on the Christian boys is wholesome when they are brought up in the midst of the open competition which they will have to meet in after life. Thus we have seen in some important colleges of the Church Missionary Society and the London Missionary Society that the chief aim has been somewhat modified so as to make them primarily places for the training of Christian youths, but the advantages of the institutions are thrown open to non-Christians as well. But a good number of high schools and colleges are attended largely, some almost exclusively, by non-Christians; and many of th: best institutions, such as the Madras Christian College, are maintained primarily for those classes, and our discussion in the remainder of this chapter will deal with a consideration of educational missions as affecting the non-Christian community.

Some people would find fault with the missionary for having any other immediate aim than the conversion of the people. It is only as the teaching of mathematics and science can contribute to convincing men of the truth of the gospel that they are considered useful subjects; while others look upon these branches as a sort of necessary and evil part of the work, forced upon mission schools by the Government, or else adopted by them as a sop or a bait to get unwary children and young people under the influences of distinctly Christian teaching and so, perchance, to bring about their conversion to Christ. Such a view was maintained by some missionary educators, many years ago, while occasionally we meet with people who write or talk about educational missions with nearly such opinions. But those who are now engaged in this work, almost without exception, would seriously repudiate such a view. While yielding to none in earnestness of persuasion that the people of India must be told the good news of salvation and need to believe in Christ, yet the aim of missionary education is not simply to make as many converts as possible. The objects of this great work may be considered from two aspects, educational and evangelistic. Educational missionaries are many of them enthusiastic educationalists, who believe in the value of educational work, anywhere under any conditions. Their ambition is to educate and to spread education; to train the human mind, whether of the little child, whose intellect is just beginning to bud forth, or of the mature scholar, whose mind scours the infinities of science and philosophy. As such they aim to secure the very best equipments and the highest efficiency in their work from an educational standpoint, and in this respect they carry on a zealous rivalry with government and native institutions. Missionaries have striven hard, and have succeeded in larger measure than other educators in India, in correcting some of the abuses attendant on the examination system, and they have given their students high ideals of life. They believe that by including religious knowledge and moral training in their curriculum they are giving their students a broader course and a better preparation for life. Realizing how wide the field is and how great the need, how much of dense ignorance and illiteracy there is among the masses of the people, and how few are the workers, they are ready to welcome and assist all efforts on the part of Government or the Indians themselves in the spread of all sorts of useful learning.

Nevertheless, they are not educators merely, they are missionaries also, preachers of the gospel of Christ, and this office they hold not in opposition or contradiction to their educational office. They believe that their educational work is furthering the progress of the kingdom of God, that all true enlightenment can be used by God in his service. But while they are laboring to train the minds and the bodies of their students, they do not neglect their spiritual nature And they are zealous in this part of their undertaking all the more that they realize the great need of it and the lack of it in the secular, non-religious system, of government education. The aim of educational missionaries is to teach the life and knowledge of Christ, and to seek by lawful persuasion to bring their students to take him as their teacher and saviour. The opportunities of the educational missionary are wonderful in this direction. * He is the acknowledged teacher and friend of hundreds of young men and boys, whom he meets daily in the friendly intercourse of the class-room, and in the less formal association of the playground. They seek his advice in their literary societies, where he is often asked to preside, and they come to his home, if invited, and there are entertained by his books, pictures on the walls, and perhaps by the missionary's wife playing on the piano. They respond to heart to heart talks on matters of religion, which is always a subject of profound interest to them. Needless to say, there is a danger of being sentimental, which the wise missionary will avoid, using tact and common sense, and commending thus the cause he represents. The educational missionary is, then, a teacher of secular and divine things, and also a winner of souls.

But there is still another aspect of his work which needs to be considered, regarded by many as the most important. From this view educational agencies are

---

* See Wilder: Among India's Students.

preparatory, preparing the way for the triumph of the gospel in India. * We observe that God's way, both in nature and in grace, is to make large use of preparatory instrumentality. We see this clearly in the history of such a nation as Israel, but also more or less plainly in all human history. God's servants have often acted on the principle that subordinate preparatory agencies are to be employed in the mighty task of uplifting mankind. Such are the principles according to which educational missions are carried on. Dr. Miller thus speaks of the aims of the Scottish church, which inaugurated this movement: "Both in its theory and its practice, that church maintains that while the simple presentation of the message of forgiveness and love through the cross of Christ is the highest form of Christian effort and the central means of building up the church, there is yet, according to the divine plan, both room and need for humbler agencies to work in auxiliary subordination to it. That church's aim has been to lay herself along the line of the divine purpose, and to do intentionally, and therefore more rapidly, a work that must be done somehow if the divine purposes are to be fully carried out......With views like these, schools and colleges were established. In these the minds were to be formed and trained of those who were within the Hindu community and who could not fail to affect that community in all its thoughts and ways. In such institutions all truth that could help to form thought and character aright was to be inculcated as opportunity served, and all to be so inculcated as to set in the forefront that revelation of love which is the key

* See Dr. Miller: Educational Agencies in Missions, World's Congress of Missions, Chicago, 1893; also, The Place of Christian Education in The Story of India, Madras Christian College Magazine, April, 1896.

to human history and the germ of all true progress. As the most important among truths of this kind, the words of Scripture, and especially the words of Christ, were to be studied. The Scriptures were to be the spear-head, all other knowlege the well-fitted handle. The Scriptures were to be the healing essence, all other knowledge the congenial medium through which it is conveyed ...... The aim of those who work in this way is to be instruments in helping and hastening the changes in the thoughts, and character, and tendencies of men, which are necessary, according to the ordinary government of the world, for the thorough accomplishment of God's great design."

On this basis there is no doubt in the minds of those engaged in educational work that it is one of the most potent forces that are at work to revolutionize India. For it is the aim of Christian colleges all over India, educating thousands of young men and considerable numbers of young women, to communicate to these the deepest principles of right conduct. They seek to awaken and direct the moral feeling and to mould the characters of their students, so that they will love the truth when it is presented to them, and that they will be courageous enough to do their full duty as they see it, and willing to deny themselves every convenience for the sake of principle. They aim to inculcate the truth that God rules the world according to a wise and generous purpose, which may be apprehended, at least partially, by man, and to which we all ought to conform, and in which it is our highest privilege to co-operate. To this end, especially, the distinctly religious and moral teaching is directed, seeking to show what is known concerning this all-embracing divine plan. God's peculiar dealings with the nation of Israel serve as a fitting object lesson of the methods used by the Father in heaven for reclaiming his perverse and yet beloved children. But the most clear manifestation of the divine plan is shown in the words and life and death of Jesus of Nazareth, whose thoughts and guidance the world can never outgrow, who is coming, more and more, to be accepted as the teacher and inspirer of the lives and conduct of Indian youth. Dr. Miller says: "We believe that even those who may not accept the whole of what we teach will find in what they do accept, if even a little of it makes its way into their hearts, a source of purer, fuller, nobler life than could ever have been theirs without it."

The aim of missionary education has, then, to be regarded as three-fold; namely, the purely educational, the evangelistic, and the preparatory: and there is danger that any one of them may be over-emphasized and the others neglected. The task laid upon the educational missionary is a united one, and all parts of his work, including the so-called secular, are truly missionary, and together form a whole of which no part is to be sacrificed to any other. "He has put into his hands the plastic mind and character of non-Christian youths and he is responsible, in the measure in which they are under his care, for the kind of men they will be when they are grown up and have taken their place in the world; for what they will make of life and what life will make of them. The Hindu parent, on the one hand, may regard the Scripture lesson as waste of time, and value the school only for its secular instruction; and the Christian supporter of missions may sometimes, on the other hand, tend to depreciate the secular, and to regard the hours spent over the Bible as the object of all the educational apparatus; but the teacher himself must not be drawn aside to either of these errors. If he is betrayed into maintaining in his own idea and practice the current separation between the *secular* and *religious* sides of his work, if he regards or treats five-sixths of the school curriculum as a bait to secure an audience for the Scripture lesson, if he measures the results of his work solely by the number of converts won among his pupils, or by the steps they take on the road toward conversion, he comes grievously short of the right standard....The calling of the teacher is as sacred and as little to be made a mere instrument, even of the highest purposes, as that of the doctor....I make bold to believe that, along with him who gives a cup of cold water to one of these little ones, he who in the name and for the sake of Christ teaches them even the multiplication table, has blessed them with Christian blessing, and will in no wise lose his reward.

"Let the religious and secular be regarded as allies instead of opponents: let them be as the vessel of gold and the vessel of brass, both sacred to the service of the sanctuary, and then the benefit of either is the benefit of both. Let the educational missionary recognize that the task assigned him by Christ is to transform by all the means the school affords the whole nature of the pupils committed to his care; and let the same lesson be impressed on all workers in the educational field, down to the humblest teacher in the primary school, and then in the day when the history of the Christianization of India comes to be written, it will be manifest beyond a doubt that in that great process missionary education has rendered splendid and invaluable service." *

* Findlay: Decennial Missionary Conference, Bombay, 1892-93.

CHAPTER II.

THE RESULTS OF MISSIONARY EDUCATION.

From a consideration of the subject of the previous chapter it may be inferred that the outcome or results of missionary education will not always be easy to trace or define. If the aim were simply to make converts, or if it were to produce as many graduates as possible, or to accomplish some other tangible thing that could be measured or counted, our task would then plainly be to number the converts or otherwise measure up the work; and we could then judge whether the task contemplated had been efficiently carried out or not. But as we have seen, we are dealing with spiritual and invisible forces, and the object of educational missions has been to influence these, and to bring about results that can only be observed by a careful and comprehensive study of powerful movements that are often hidden from the eyes of the careless looker on. Much of the result of the great work of missionary education has already been traced in the History of the movement, and particularly in the last chapter of the History it has appeared how very large is the work, and what marvellous numerical results have been attained. It is the purpose of this chapter, not so much to speak of the general and educational results of the work, but to indicate what are the unique and distinct results especially with reference to the broad moral and spiritual aims set forth in the previous chapter.

Christian education in India, so far as it affects the non-Christian community, is dealing with the highest and most important classes of the people. Whatever it accomplishes here is sure to affect largely the destiny of the Indian nation: for though history records many conspicuous and brilliant examples of persons of low birth who have become great and have powerfully influenced their generation, it would be a fallacy to suppose that the lives of slaves and peasants are more important than the higher classes in the growth and progress of the nation. Among these classes of the people of India, who have held sway over the hearts and minds, as well as over the bodies and property, of all the others for thousands of years, what has Christian education accomplished?

1. *It has imparted true notions of Christianity, of its teachings and purposes.* The missionary who goes out into the streets of the cities and towns, as a rule, reaches very few of the higher classes, and the occasion does not often lend itself to a systematic exposition of truth. If he attempted this very few would have the patience to listen, and in fact, his audience is a fluctuating one, people coming and going all the time, and very few staying from the beginning to the end of a discourse, so that he is addressing people as it were in a procession. Nor does he habitually meet the same people from day to day. But in a Christian school or college the Bible and the truths of Christianity are taught systematically, day after day, and month after month, to the same pupils. They come when they are young, often very young, and stay for years, sometimes twenty years, in Christian schools. Many non-Christian pupils and graduates of missionary institutions actually know more of the Bible than the majority of Christian people in a Christian land. The following is a copy of a test set for three months work in a college class:—

(1). Quote as nearly as possible the first prophecy

concerning Jesus Christ. Where is it referred to in the New Testament? Explain fully its meaning and state what you know about its fulfilment.

(2). Quote some important verses from Isaiah's prophecy concerning Jesus. When was it written? In what respect is it superior to other prophecies?

(3). Tell what is meant by vicarious atonement. Explain: The Lord hath laid on him the iniquity of us all.

(4). Give as much as you know of the life of Matthew. For whom did he write his Gospel? State some of the peculiar features of his Gospel.

(5). Tell all you know about the author of the third Gospel: His birth, parentage, training and later life. Did he ever see Christ?

(6). For whom was Luke's Gospel written? To what class or condition of people is it especially applicable? Prove this by examples. What other special things do you notice about this Gospel?

(7). Give a complete and accurate account of the announcement of the birth (a) of John, (b) of Jesus. Contrast Zechariah's and Mary's reception of the angel's word.

(8). Give the full meaning of John's baptism, and tell why Jesus was both circumcised and baptized.

(9). Give the context and full meaning of:—He shall give his angels charge concerning thee; Make ye ready the way of the Lord; The LORD hath said unto my Lord.

In the Report of the Wilson College for 1905, which has Christian as well as non-Christian students, it is stated: "The Alexander Miller prizes for Scripture were won, the first by a Hindu student, the second by a Parsee student. The papers in this competition which I examined showed in the case of a considerable number of students the result of careful attention to the work done during the year, and a very intelligent grasp of Scripture truth."

2. *Christian education creates feelings of friendliness*

amongst the higher classes towards the missionaries and also towards the religion which they represent. Numerous instances could be given of the friendliness and help bestowed by ex-pupils of mission schools upon both missionaries and Indian Christians. At the Bangalore Conference, held in 1879, Mr. Hudson told the following incident: "Entering a certain village the priest assured us that we could tell them nothing worth knowing, and when we tried to speak some hooted and others walked off. As we were about to leave, another Brahman just entered the village, and he was one who had been educated in the mission school at Bangalore. He shook hands with the missionary and invited him to his house, and then learning of the reception we had just received, he sharply rebuked his people and apologized to the missionary for their conduct. We have visited that village every week since then, and opposition has given way to earnest attention." We ourselves have heard a Brahman district judge in the presence of a non-Christian audience publicly commend the reading and study of the Bible, and he bore testimony to the fact that ever since he had attended a Scotch mission school, thirty years before, he had continued in the daily habit of reading the Bible. Such men are found all over India, occupying prominent positions and representing the most thoughtful portion of the non-Christian community. The interest that is felt in Bible study among non-Christians is indicated by the fact that one of their number, a learned advocate in Ceylon, has recently published a commentary on Matthew's and John's Gospels. The following testimony of a gifted Hindu ascetic is quoted by the Rev. T. E. Slater: "There is no ideal of life so pure and lofty as that found in your New Testament, and no example so holy and sweet as is given in the character of your Christ. I find my greatest comfort and inspiration when I turn to that book and read of him." Such testimonies are numerous.

3. *Christian education has proved the best means of winning converts from the higher classes.* An objection of considerable force often heard made against educational agencies in missions is that they are barren of results as seen in conversions of students. We have already seen how numerous were the converts in the early years of educational effort, and what was the quality of some of these men who have been leaders in the Indian church till this time. Nowadays, though the work is carried on so much more extensively, the professed converts are far fewer, and many reasons have been given to explain this fact, which need not be entered upon here. It remains to point out that almost all the converts that do come at all these days from the higher classes come by means of the school or college, so that this form of work is still the best means to this end. Nor are the converts by any means so few as is sometimes thought. On a careful reading of hundreds of mission reports, published by various societies within the last few years, we were surprised at the large number of converts reported from the schools. The Report of a single society, the Church Missionary Society, for last year, gave instances of nearly fifty baptisms of school pupils from non-Christian homes. It is certain that there are hundreds such every year throughout India. One Report stated that nearly all their converts came directly or indirectly through means of the schools. Even approximately accurate statistics are not available, and if they were, they would bring out only a small fraction of the work accomplished by Christian education, which is largely a work of preparation.

4. *Christian education has imparted a new spirit and new ideals to Hindu life itself.* Just as in the days of the Protestant Reformation there occurred a counter-reformation, so Hinduism has been revived, and numerous organizations have been formed that have imbibed the spirit of Christian teaching. The various Samajes and assemblies for prayer and religious study among young men, such as the Young Men's Hindu Association, bear testimony to this spirit. These nearly all have the Bible, as well as the Koran and the Vedas, as their subjects of study, and in a sense they all honor Jesus Christ, and profess to admire above all things his matchless precepts. It is significant that many of the leaders of such societies are graduates and ex-pupils from mission colleges. Dr. Ewing, Principal of the Forman Christian College, wrote recently in the Harvest Field: "In the strongest center of the Arya Samaj in India the President and the Secretary of the one party and the Secretary of the other are graduates of the Forman College." The Arya Samaj makes much of its professed admiration of the Vedas, yet in a conversation, not long ago, with an ardent member of that body, we found that he had never read one word of the Vedas, either in translation or in the original, though he was tolerably familiar with the Bible. In general, the highest ideals which the most sincere young men feel and express are not found to be obtained from the Hindu Shastras but from the Christian Scriptures. Only a short time ago a public assembly was opened in Calcutta with a solemn public prayer by the editor of a leading Hindu daily in language quite Christian. Many of the better class journals edited by Hindus are filled with distinctly Christian references, direct quotations from Scripture, and applications without reserve from the teachings of Jesus. Just how far these

conditions can be traced specifically to Christian educational work, as distinguished from other Christian agencies, is hard to determine, yet there can be no doubt that the way in which mission schools have made the Bible familiar to the upper classes has had a tremendous leavening influence on their society.

5. *The teaching of the Bible has had a sound moral influence on the life of students of Christian schools.* Government educational authorities have felt the need from the very beginning of some form of moral education in the public system, but have found none because they dared not sanction the use of the Bible. Recent government utterances have already been quoted containing reference to this matter. At a recent annual prize distribution at the Church Mission high school at Jubbulpore, Sir Anthony P. Mac Donnell, K.C.S.I., Civil Commissioner of the Central Provinces, presided, and in the course of his address, in which he referred to the difficulties which beset the Government in the attempt to convey moral training in state schools, remarked: "For my own part, I consider that the problem can alone be solved by such institutions as this, which are free to make religious and moral teaching part of the daily curriculum."* Non-Christian parents have felt the same way, and hence some of them prefer to send their sons to a Christian school, rather than to one where there is no moral education whatever. The actual result in this case is difficult to estimate, yet it is certain that Christian education has done much to raise the standard of morality and of justice in Indian courts, where the judge as well as the lawyers have been under its influ-

*Quoted by Dr. Dennis, Christian Missions and Social Progress, Volume. I. p. 360.

ence; and also in every department of home and commercial life.

6. *Christian education has had a large and growing influence on the social progress of India.* This is especially seen in the destruction of caste and in the elevation of women. Christian missions were the pioneers in female education, and even to-day they are the most successful in this kind of effort, as also the Education Commission of 1882 testified. Christian education has exerted a unique influence on the political and national life, which in the present crisis may prove the saving of India. The reports from mission colleges of 1905 and 1906 refer very largely to a social and political unrest manifest among students, and to the way in which missionary educators have met these conditions. Difficulties have increased but on the whole the schools have had a steadying influence upon the life of young India.

Finally, referring once more to the distinctly religious influence of Christian education, it has brought a large proportion of the best classes of men and women to the feet of the great Teacher and we believe they are learning of him. As the late lamented Dr. Samuel Satthianadhan wrote in a recent article of the *Missionary Review of the World*: "The personality of Christ is laying hold of the heart and mind of India with an irresistible and growing power." What the results are and may become in the future of missionary education in India, they depend absolutely on the measure in which it is subject to the mind and spirit of Him in whose name it is carried on.

We conclude this chapter with a few selected testimonies to the value of educational missions: these will include, first, the evidence of representatives of the

Government of India; second, the testimony of missionary conferences in India, as voicing the united sentiments of those working on the field, engaged not only in educational but also in other forms of missionary work; and lastly, the opinion of travellers and students of mission work in the home land.

Sir William Muir, K.C.S.I., D.C.L., LL.D., Secretary to the Government of India, Lieutenant-Governor of the North West Provinces, said in a letter to a committee of the Church of Scotland: "I have no hesitation whatever in saying that it would be a calamity for India if missionary schools were withdrawn. Apart from immediate conversion to the faith, their influence on the mind of the people has been of inestimable value." In 1887, Lord Dufferin, then Viceroy of India, in reviewing the whole position, thus sums up in his Minute on Education: "In aided schools religious instruction may, of course, be freely given, and the Governor-General in Council would be sincerely glad if the number of aided schools and colleges in which religious instruction is prominently recognized were largely increased. It is in this direction that the best solution of this difficult problem can be found."

Turning now to what the missionaries have to say on the matter, in 1879, the following Resolution was passed, without a single dissenting voice, by the Bangalore Conference, representing all the Missions in South India.

"This Conference desires to express its full appreciation of the value of high class Christian education as a missionary agency, and its hope that friends of Indian missions will sympathise with this equally with other branches of evangelistic work in this country. The Indian church needs at present, and will still more need in the future, men of superior education to occupy positions of trust and responsibility as pastors, evangelists, and leading members of the community, such as can only be supplied by our high class Christian institutions. Those missionaries who are engaged in *vernacular work* desire especially to bear testimony to the powerful effect in favor of Christianity which those institutions are exercising throughout the country, and to record their high regard for the *educational work* as a necessary part of the work of the Christian church in India. This Conference feels bound to place on record its conviction that these two great branches of Christian work are indispensable complements of one another, and would earnestly hope that they will be so regarded by the Christian church, and that both will meet with continued and hearty support."

The Decennial Conference, representing all missionary societies in the whole of India, which met in Madras in 1902, declared :—

"The Conference recognizes that the Christian instruction given in open missionary institutions is essentially evangelistic, and it puts on record its opinion that no line is drawn or can be drawn between educational and evangelistic work ......The Conference, recognizing the unique opportunity which mission colleges possess of evangelizing those classes which are largely inaccessible to other methods of missionary agency, would hope that this declaration of their opinion may lead to the establishment of mission colleges in all large centres of population, the principle of co-operation being observed, wherever possible."

Lastly, of students of missions in the home-land, we shall find the best representatives to be the Rev. J. S. Dennis, D.D., Dr. Gustav Warneck, and Mr. John R. Mott. These men, having approached the study of the subject of Christian missions, each from a different standpoint, have arrived at practically the same conclusion, regarding the position of missionary education. Dr. Dennis, traveller and scholar, having seen for himself the work of missions in many lands, and author of that scholarly work in four volumes on *Christian Missions and Social Progress*, gives emphatic testimony to the value of educational missions. Among much else he says :—"The inestimable value of Christian education as a factor in the higher progress of India is apparent" "The valuable opportunity which educational work gives for special efforts among students, and among the educated classes in general, is apparent." "Its power to reach all grades of Indian society is also noticeable." "The contribution of moral character which education makes to Indian society is another of the striking evidences of its social value." *

Dr. Warneck, a German theologian and scholar, who has worked out very carefully in his *Missions-Lehre*, in four volumes, the whole theory of missions, devotes an important chapter to this subject. Every phase of the question, its New Testament basis, education for Christians and non-Christians, primary and higher education, the pros and the cons, are all carefully considered. He says that "The importance of mission schools can scarcely be over-estimated." "They have a very great influence on the coming generation, and hence on the whole life of the people." Speaking of the difficulties of reaching the high caste Hindu, on account of the subtlety of his thought and his pantheistic philosophy, he says: "If anywhere on the misson field, then surely in India, conversion needs a preparation, and mission schools claim nothing more than to be a means which pave the way for the understanding of the preaching of salvation, and for making this preaching of powerful effect. Without a revolution in thought, such as can be accomplished only by Christian education, a wide-spread Christian movement among the Hindu people can scarcely come." †

---

* Dennis, "Christian Missions and Social Progress," Vol. III., pp. 29-32.

† Warneck, *Missions-Lehre* Vol. III., Part 2, pp. 155-158.

But perhaps no traveller or scholar has had such opportunities of observing the influence of missionary education along with other lines of Christian work in foreign lands as Mr. John R. Mott, M.A., F.R.G.S., who has made more than one world-tour of nearly all the fields, and has spent many months in direct work among students of many different nations and creeds, and has organized student conferences, and established Young Men's Christian Associations and Bible-study classes among them. In *Stategic Points in the World's Conquest,* he says:—"The work of educational missions in India is of transcendant importance. Not a few are disposed to look upon educational mission work as less important than directly evangelistic work. We had shared this feeling. A careful study of the question in four or five mission countries, however, has led us to attach the greatest possible importance to educational missions. No country has done more to deepen this conviction than India. Educational missions have opened a larger number of doors for the preaching of the gospel than any other agency. They have furnished the most distinguished and influential converts, and have done more than all else combined to undermine heathen superstitions and false systems of belief. They are to-day the chief, if not the only, force to counteract the influence of the secular character and tendency of the government institutions of learning."*

---

* pp. 96-108.

CHAPTER III.

PROBLEMS AND NEEDS OF MISSIONARY EDUCATION.

In the past and present conduct of missionary education there have always arisen many problems that have been difficult of solution. A statement of some of the most fundamental of these questions and some solutions in the light of past experience will be attempted.

1. *Christian or non-Christian Teachers.* A great deal of controversy has been waged around this point, and the extreme position has been strenuously defended that in Christ's work none but his own servants should be employed. There is no doubt that this is thc ideal condition, and it seems so palpable that many even to-day cannot understand how any other views or practice can be tolerated. Two very important difficulties arose from the very beginning, and continue till this day with scarcely diminishing force. In the first place, it has been altogether impossible to get a sufficient number of well-trained Christian teachers; and secondly, non-Christian parents have been loath to send their children to schools where all the instructors are Christians. This is especially true in the case of high caste Hindu and Muhammadan girls. Now it has been found that in many instances non-Christian teachers have proved very serviceable in teaching secular subjects, and where Christian forces are so few it is well that they be conserved for specifically religious work, and not have all their time taken up with secular teaching. It has also

been found that by employing non-Christian teachers in mission schools they, as well as the pupils, have come under the influence of the gospel. The first convert of the London Missionary Society in Coimbatore was a high caste Hindu, who had been employed as a teacher in a mission school, not only of secular branches, but of Watt's Catechism, and the Bible.*

How early this problem was felt may be seen from a letter of Dr. John Wilson, to the Committee of the Scottish Church, in which he says: "I can well sympathise with any mind still entertaining these difficulties. I do not think them insurmountable when the real order of procedure of our schools is attended to. Our heathen teachers bind themselves to abstain from teaching heathenism in our schools; and from a close inspection of them, I believe they do so abstain......Four of our teachers have been baptized since the commencement of our mission, and an encouraging number of the pupils." Wilder, in his book on *Mission Schools in India*, quotes many instances of conversions among teachers. Such cases are reported in last year's reports. This is not said, however, to minimize the need for Christian teachers, or to withdraw attention from the danger that may sometimes occur to the work by the employment of non-Christian teachers. There is no doubt that the greatest need of missionary education to-day is for Christian teachers of high standing. Where a Christian of low caste extraction, and of no academic qualifications, comes in for an hour a day to teach a class that for the remainder of the time is under the guidance of a cultured non-Christian teacher, in the subjects wherein the class is most interested, we cannot expect much good to come from it. The Christian teacher

* Lovett: History of the L.M.S., Vol. II, p. 85.

must be well qualified in secular knowledge, and should actually teach some secular subject in the school. The time so spent is not lost, for it is only thus that his standing in the school and influence over the pupils can be maintained.

The following statistics give the numbers of Christian and non-Christian teachers employed in mission schools during the last four decades, and show that the number and percentage of Christian teachers is increasing in an encouraging way :—

Year.	Christian.	Non-Christian.	Percentage Christian.
1871	1901	2206	47
1881	3841	2462	61
1891	5207	3132	63
1901	8670	3278	73

It would be well if we could know that there has been a similar growth in quality; this is probable, though the growth has been largest in the lower grades. The one thing to which attention must be directed in succeeding years is to raise up Christian teachers. This is not simply to be accomplished by establishing mission training schools, but by encouraging Christian boys and girls to climb higher and higher on the educational ladder, and by sending as many Christian students as possible to training schools that already exist. The Decennial Conference, Madras, 1902, recommended the following : "Henceforward it appears to us that provision for training of Christian masters, and securing greater efficiency, must at least go hand-in-hand with extension of the work." *

Another great need in line with the above is the

* Report, p. 84.

provision of more American and European missionary teachers in connection with higher mission institutions. These are somewhat more expensive than Indian Christian graduates, but so long as the latter are so scarce there is a prime necessity for furnishing as many foreign teachers as possible. Quite apart from this, we believe that there is no field where the foreign missionary can exert a better influence than in the schools, and perhaps long after his usefulness might be questioned in pastoral and evangelistic work among the Indian people, his position as a teacher in colleges and schools will still be a recognized need. At a summer school in Japan, attended by about four hundred Japanese ministers and teachers, one of the conclusions reached was :—

> "We do not deem it necessary that many more missionaries should be sent us from America to preach the gospel to the masses of our people. The ordinary work of preaching can be done quite as well by educated men of our own race. But if our friends across the ocean can send us men, able to teach us how we may grapple with rival systems of religion or philosophy, and all the burning questions which confront us, then the more they send the better." *

The ideal requirement would be one missionary teacher for each class in college, and one for each high school, whether that is connected with a college or not. It is needless to point out that educational missionaries should be men of broad scholarship, and well qualified for teaching their special subjects. The Decennial Conference, Madras, 1902, passed the following Resolution : "The Conference would press upon Mission Committees the necessity of seeing that educational missionaries are trained to teach. The educational missionary must henceforth be regarded much more as a specialist, like

* Quoted by Dr. F. F. Ellinwood, Conference of Foreign Mission Boards, January, 1894.

the medical and artisan missionary, requiring a preliminary training in his specialty." *

2. *The place of religious teaching in mission schools.* From the beginning it has been the aim of those engaged in this work to make it a strong evangelistic force, and religious teaching has always held a high place in the curriculum. The danger is growing more and more that, owing on the one hand, to the strong pressure of Government in everything belonging to the secular side of the school, and, on the other hand, to the engrossing interest that the mass of students have for the education that will help them to pass their examinations and to get on in the world, religious matters will lose their hold on the attention of both teachers and pupils. It must be recognized that mere compulsion is not apt to make the subject attractive, or to do much good in any way; and the missionaries in charge of educational institutions must use much tact to secure for this subject the interest which it deserves to have. Dr. Miller speaks thus hopefully of this subject at the All-India Decennial Conference, Calcutta, 1882: "No complaint has ever reached me of the four best hours of the student's week being devoted to subjects that count for nothing in the university examinations. ...... Careful attention, lively energetic teaching, are essential to keep things right in any class; but these things when they are present result in attention, in careful preparation, in intelligent interest, in regard to Scripture quite as certainly and quite as easily as in regard to any other subject." The things that will help to this end are that religious education be given a foremost place in the school, and be held up as important. Enthusiasm is

* Report, pp. 85, 86.

communicative, and the missionary can easily impart his zeal to his school. The best teachers must be employed for religious subjects, who will make their teaching interesting and worth while. Then also, a system of prizes will encourage certain numbers and will help to place religious teaching on a proper footing in its relation to other subjects, in which there are often numerous and valuable prizes. It is customary in nearly all mission schools to require all the students to assemble in the morning to attend Scripture reading and prayer. We have already seen what the practice of the earliest Christian college was in this respect. (p. 12.) It is questionable if the forced attendance at public prayer on the part of Hindu and Muhammadan students who are out of sympathy with the exercises will do any good.

There is a general consensus of opinion and unity of practice which makes the Bible the chief and only text-book in this department. Knowledge of the Bible is held to be more important than that of any synopsis of evidences or catechism; but there is need of outlines and a careful marking out of courses; and of normal training of teachers, as well as frequent inspection of their work. The question of what Readers to use in Christian schools is of much importance in this connection. The man who has done Herculean service in this cause, Dr. John Murdoch, has always pleaded powerfully and sometimes pathetically for the books that the Christian Literature Society has sent out from year to year. The early educational missionaries were the first to write and edit school books adapted to India, and the religious lessons in these were considered important. Says Dr. John Anderson: "And next to the inculcation of the Word of God itself would we place the Christian school book, as an instrument for good." * All the pioneers were agreed on this matter. But of late years, for various reasons, there has been a change. In an *Appeal to Missionaries*, written in 1899, Dr. Murdoch says: "The writer is now in his eightieth year. He is one of the few survivors who knew Dr. Duff, Dr. Wilson, Dr. Anderson, etc. The retrospect is not altogether pleasing. There are large institutions in which the Christian Readers in use forty years ago have been swept away, and replaced by others from which either every Christian reference has been entirely excluded, or which have only a few allusions, few and far between." The reason is not far to seek. Some really good Readers have been provided by Government, from which the subject of religion is of course excluded. Inspectors, mostly non-Christian, have favored these books. A strong conscientious objection is made by some missionaries that Christian Readers cannot be taught by non-Christian teachers, and it is argued that while the Bible and Christian evidences should be taught and placed in the foreground in all mission schools, they should not be sandwiched in between and in connection with the regular lesson in spelling or grammar. The compilers of the Christian series have felt the force of this, and in their "Directions to Teachers" prefixed to their Readers they expressly assert: "Religious lessons should, in no case, be used for spelling or grammar. The teacher should only ascertain, in a becoming manner, that the pupils understand the sense."

3. *The Harmony of Christian Education with the Aims of the People.* It is important to consider the question of how far missionaries are fitting their pupils for life in their environment, always an important

---

*In the *Native Herald,* October, 1841.

question in education. At a non-Christian social conference, held this year in Cocanada, India, the President referred in the following terms to the system of education, not missionary education alone, in vogue in India :—

"The education we are receiving is different from that which the preceding generations have received and also from that which we all receive at home. The old order had in it the merit that there was no antagonism between education and home influences. What the teacher taught was reflected in every-day life. The new order presents a moral and mental chaos. What the universities set before the young man, the home life contradicts and the boy grows up with opinions which his early associations have done nothing to convert into real living convictions ...... The result is inconsistency between the conduct and the conviction of the man who is brought up under this dual system, the adoption of opinions which do not influence the growth of conduct, which is not balanced by any well-formed consistent set of principles...... His life is a bundle of inconsistencies; he is one thing at home, another thing outside." *

If this is true of state education, it is more strikingly true of missionary education; yet it cannot be urged that we seek to diminish the contrast, but the necessity of reckoning with it is great. It is quite true that missionaries are trying to educate the young generation of India, both boys and girls, to be superior to much of their surroundings, to be better and cleaner and purer in speech and in thought, than naturally they would have been brought up to. They are trying to teach them not to live the double life referred to in the quotation above; but realizing what their home influences are, they should be conciliatory in the extreme, nor should anything be done that would detract in the minds of the pupils from the sacredness of home.

The following extract from an editorial published in

* The Indian Social Reformer, May 19,1907.

The Hindu, a leading Indian daily of South India, is concerned with this subject and shows the light in which many non-Christians now regard the religious instruction given in mission schools. The article is a strange mixture of praise and blame :—

"We believe that no reasonable person, or body of persons, who have any respect for human liberty, can possibly hold it just that boys should be compelled to receive instruction of a kind to which their parents seriously object...... While therefore we are duly thankful to our Christian missionary friends for all their earnest labor and zeal on our behalf, we shall be wanting in our duty to ourselves as well as to our friends, if we any longer conceal from them the growing desire on the part of a very large majority, in fact, the entire thinking portion of the Indian population, to provide educational opportunities for their children without sacrificing their conscience ...... Thanks to the sincere and whole hearted labors of the missionaries themselves, the social conscience has been aroused. (Note these words) ...... It is with no small pleasure that we testify to the fact that in the largest and best of the Christian educational institutions in this part of the country, the Christian religious instruction, compulsory though it has been, has to a very large extent been managed with due regard to the sentiments of the students......In this work the noble band of scholarly teachers of that institution have, in the opinion of most of its alumni, who still cherish the warmest appreciation of the lessons they have learned in their college days, eminently succeeded ......We are prepared to concede that there are quite a number of Christian teachers in this country who have earned the love and reverence of their pupils." *

4. *Need of Extension.* One of the greatest problems before the missionary body in this work, the easiest to solve on paper, but hard to answer actually, is how to increase the educational work to make it adequate to the great needs of the country. We have seen from the statistics what is being done : over 500,000 in Christian schools.

---

* *The Hindu*, November 19th, 1904.

The Government and various agencies are educating enough to make the total number of pupils and students in schools and colleges, nearly four and a half million. At a ratio of fifteen per cent. to the total population there are at least ten times as many children of school-going age, or 45,000,000. In the case of girls only about one-fortieth of those of school-going age are in school: in other words, while there are nearly half a million girls in all schools, there are more than twenty-two million who ought to be there. To see how little is being done from another point of view, we may note that the amount of money spent annually in all India, by Government, native agencies, and missionary societies combined, is nearly $13,000,000 for 300,000,000 people; while about an equal amount is spent in the State of Michigan for public schools alone, for *two and a half* million people.

Now it is not thought for a moment that the responsibility for educating the children of India rests on the missionary societies. The above figures rather call attention to the duty of the Government of India, whose responsibility has been acknowledged by such Viceroys as Lord Curzon. But while the conditions thus revealed do not imply a direct obligation, yet they indicate the wide field that is still open, and that constitutes a marvellous opportunity for the Christian church in India.

But there is a department of this work in which missionaries are more directly concerned. The Rev. Mr. Andrew, in a pamphlet published by the South Indian Missionary Association, in 1904, on *The Uneducated Children of the Presidency*, makes out by a careful computation that the number of children of the Christian community in the Presidency of Madras is about 275,000; of whom, according to the Report of the Director of

Public Instruction, there are less than 64,000 in schools of any kind. This leaves 211,000 Christian children without any education whatever. * No doubt, a similar or worse story remains to be told of the other parts of India: and the vast need indicated by this situation is one that appeals with peculiar force to all who are interested in the future welfare of Christianity in India. There may be some consolation in the fact, already pointed out, that the condition of the Christian community is much better than that of the other religions.

We have chosen to consider in this chapter the double subject of Problems and Needs, because, as has become manifest, many of the needs have arisen out of the problems. It is altogether impossible to present adequately the needs of this work. They are all that a great undertaking, built on a good and solid foundation, approved by many years of experience, with an enormous field for expansion, can require in order to meet the boundless opportunity that awaits it.

The great need is for more qualified men and women as teachers. In many institutions positions have long been vacant, and nearly every college and high school is clamoring for additional forces. Money is needed for teachers' salaries and for additional buildings and equipments. The following is a partial list, published by one of the smaller colleges, of things "urgently needed."

"Five endowments of $50,000 each, for American Professors, one each, teaching: The English Language and Literature; Natural Science; Pedagogy; Theology; Industries.

"Five endowments of $10,000 to $15,000 each, for Indian Professors, one each, teaching: Mathematics; History; San-

* These figures are obtained not on the usual basis of 15 per cent., but Mr. Andrew says he took the actual number of persons in the Christian community between the ages of six and fifteen.

skrit Language and Literature; Tamil Language and Literature; Hindustani Language and Literature.

"A Library, where there is no other library in the city where the college is located, of 106,000 inhabitants.

"A Dormitory for college students.

"A Science Building with Apparatus.

"Residences for American Teachers.

A similar list could be made out for nearly every one of the fifty-two colleges now in existence, and for as many others that need to be established in the sixty cities of over 50,000 population each, still remaining without a Christian college.

STATISTICAL TABLES.

The following Abbreviations are used in these tables :—

ABCFM : American Board of Commissioners for Foreign Missions.
ABMU : American Baptist Missionary Union.
PNA : Presbyterian Church in the United States of America.
ELGS : General Synod of the Evangelical Lutheran Church in the U.S.A.
RCA : Reformed Church in America.
UP : United Presbyterian Church of North America.
ME : Methodist Episcopal Church in the United States.
CPM : Canadian Presbyterian Mission.
LMS : London Missionary Society (Congregational).
CMS : Church Missionary Society (Church of England).
WMS : Wesleyan Missionary Society (English).
SPG : Society for the Propagation of the Gospel (English High Church).
UFC : United Free Church of Scotland (Presbyterian).
CSM : Church of Scotland Missionary Society (Presbyterian).
Ind : Independent Missions.
M : Madras University.
B : Bombay University.
C : Calcutta University.
P : Punjab University.
A : Allahabad University.

The Roman figures after the names of the colleges indicate the grade of the institutions : I, First Grade ; II, Second Grade. See p. 97.

PROTESTANT CHRISTIAN COLLEGES.

	Name of Institution.	Place.	Board or Society.	Year founded.	Year affiliated.	University.	Number of Foreign Missionary Teachers.	Number of Students in College Dept.
1.	American College, II	Madura	ABCFM	1880	1881	M	3	39
2.	Jaffna College, I	Ceylon	do.	1872	1893	C	4	105
3.	American Baptist Mission C., II	Ongole	ABMU	1877	1893	M	2	28
4.	Rangoon Baptist College, II	Rangoon	do.	1872	1894	C	6	26
5.	Forman Christian College, I	Lahore	PNA	1866	1888	P	4	403
6	Christian College, I	Allahabad	do.	1846	1903	A	3	104
7.	Woodstock College, II	Mussoorie	do.	1854	1901	A	8	29
8.	American Lutheran Mission C., II	Guntur	ELGS	1874	1885	M	1	69
9.	Elizabeth R. Voorhees C., II	Vellore	RCA	1868	1898	M	1	18
10.	Gordon Mission College, I	Rawalpindi	UP	1893	1895	P	3	56
11.	Reid Christian College, I	Lucknow	ME	1877	1888	A	3	87
12.	Isabella Thoburn College. I	Lucknow	do.	1870	1885	A	6	20
13.	Philander Smith College, II	Naini Tal	do.	1880	1891	A	2	12
14.	Canadian Mission College, I	Indore	CPM	1884	1888	A	4	47
15.	L.M.S. Institution, I	Bhowanipur	LMS	1837	1857	C	4	97
16.	Ramsay College, II	Almora	do.	1850	1885	A	2	31
17.	Scott Christian College, II	Nagercoil	do.	1821	1893	M	1	37
18.	Wardlaw Clollege, II	Bellary	do.	1846	1891	M	0	12
19.	Noble C olege, I	Masulipatam	CMS	1843	1877	M	3	92
20.	St. John's College, I	Agra	do.	1853	1862	A	6	175

21.	Trinity College, II *	Kandy	CMS	1872	1878	...	2	...
22.	Church Mission College, II	Kottayam	do.	1837	1892	M	2	129
23.	Church Mission College, II	Tinnevelly	do.	1878	1878	M	1	69
24.	Cathedral Mission College, II	Calcutta	do.	1865	1899	C	1	36
25.	St. Andrew's College, II	Gorakhpur	do.	...	1899	A	1	35
26.	St. John's College, II *	Jaffna	do.	1841	1892	...	2	...
27.	Sarah Tucker College, II	Palamcotta	do.	1864	1896	M	5	9
28.	St. Paul's School, I	Darjeeling	do.	1845	1857	C	7	...
29.	Edwardes Church Mission C., II	Peshawar	do.	1900	1905	P	2	24
30.	Wesleyan Mission College, II	Bankura	WMS	1903	1906	C	2	80
31.	Wesley College, II	Madras	do.	1851	1887	M	2	47
32.	Findlay College, II	Mannargudi	do.	1845	1898	M	2	87
33.	Wesleyan Central College, II *	Batticaloa	do.	1814	1877	...	1	...
34.	Wesley College, II *	Colombo	do.	1874	1876	L	2	...
35.	Central College, II	Jaffna	do.	1834	1897	C,M	2	30
36.	St. Thomas College, II *	Colombo	SPG	1840	1864	...	2	...
37.	Bishop's College, I	Calcutta	do.	1820	1860	C	3	41
38.	Christ Church College, I	Cawnpore	do.	1865	1892	A	4	55
49.	St. Peter's College, I	Tanjore	do.	1880	1880	M	1	164
40.	S.P.G. College, I	Trichinopoly	do.	1883	1889	M	3	266
41.	St. Stephen's College, I	Delhi	do.	1881	1882	P	3	110
42.	Dublin University Mission C., II	Hazaribagh	do.	1895	1899	C	6	73
43.	Duff College, I	Calcutta	UFC	1850	1857	C	6	388
44.	Wilson College, I	Bombay	do.	1835	1861	B	9	464
45.	Madras Christian College, I	Madras	do.	1837	1877	M	9	795
46.	Hislop Mission College, I	Nagpur	do.	1883	1884	A	3	110

No.	Institution	Place						
47.	General Assembly's Institution, I	Calcutta	CSM	1830	1864	C	5	643
48.	Church of Scotland Mission C., II	Madras	do.	1837	1887	M	1	114
59.	Scotch Mission College, II	Sialkot	do.	1886	1892	P	1	21
50.	Doveton College, † I	Calcutta	IND	1823	1857	C	...	18
51.	Doveton Protestant College, † II	Madras	do.	1855	1877	M	...	18
52.	City College, † II	Colombo	do.	...	...	...	0	27
	Total ...	...	...	...	...	...	156	5340

* The Colleges in Ceylon are nearly all under entirely different educational regulations and can with difficulty be classified with the other Indian colleges. Nearly all prepare their students for the Cambridge Locals, of which the Senior Examination corresponds somewhat to the Indian Intermediate or F.A. Examination.

† The last named three institutions are not properly Missionary Institutions, but they are under Protestant Christian Management.

NUMBER OF COLLEGES — HIGH SCHOOLS

Universities	Prot.	Cath.	Christian Total	Others	Total.	Prot.	Total
Calcutta	12	3	17 *	46	63	64	576
Bombay	1	1	2	10	12	16	140
Madras	17	11	28	26	54	69	249
Allahabad	11	3	14	16	30	21	76
Punjab	5	0	5	9	14	22	118
London &c.	6	0	6	0	6	0	0
Totals	52	18	72	107	179	192	1159

* This is not a mistake. Two Colleges report themselves as Christian, but neither Protestant nor Roman Catholic.

ROMAN CATHOLIC INSTITUTIONS.

1.	St. Joseph's College, II	Bangalore	1857	1882	M	12	34
2.	Sacred Heart College, II	Bangalore	1854	1902	M	1	2
3.	St. Michael's College, II	Coimbatore	1860	1892	M	2	22
4.	St. Joseph's College, II	Cuddalore	1868	1884	M	2	70
5.	Presentation Convent College, II	Madras	1884	1900	M	3	1
6.	St. Mary's Presentation Convent College, II	Madras	1892	1899	M	...	4
7.	St. Mary's College, II	Madras	1839	1883	M	3	25
8	San Thome College, II	Madras	1864	1894	M	3	14
9.	Holy Angels' Convent C., II	Trivandrum	1880	1899	M	1	...
10.	St. Aloysius College, I	Mangalore	1880	1887	M	11	43
11.	St. Joseph's College, I	Trichinopoly	1844	1877	M	14	418
12.	St. George's College, II	Mussoorie	1853	1884	A	5	...
13.	St. Peter's College, II	Agra	1845	1870	A	2	5
14.	St. Joseph's College, II	Naini Tal	...	1899	A	11	...
15.	St. Francis De Sale's School, II	Nagpur	...	1879	C	...	...
16.	St. Joseph's College, II	Darjeeling	1888	1889	C	22	...
17.	St. Xavier's College, I	Bombay	...	1869	B	12	350
18.	St. Xavier's College, I	Calcutta	1860	1862	C	14	400

GENERAL AND EDUCATIONAL STATISTICS OF VARIOUS SOCIETIES.

1 Board or Society.	2 Date established.	3 Foreign Missionaries.	4 Colleges.	5 Students in College department.	6 Preachers.	7 Teachers.	8 Churches or meeting places.	9 Schools.	10 Total pupils in all schools not Sunday Schools.	11 Sunday Schools.	12 Sunday School scholars.	13 Indian Communicant members.
ABCFM	1813	93	2	144	556	976	113	536	26221	542	19854	14354
ABMU	1814	332	2	54	1970	2251	1827	1479	41363	1084	38619	116613
PNA	1834	155	3	536	?	* 209	?	209	8564	?	9406	5487
ELGS	1842	30	1	69	256	339	481	284	8408	266	16567	11670
RCA	1853	30	1	18	213	269	164	168	7416	173	5701	2676
UP	1855	90	1	56	196	358	319	182	8708	145	6313	11159
ME	1856	278	3	119	2344	852	253	1445	37197	3201	134843	40434
CPM	1873	45	1	47	110	* 36	9	36	1343	33	1600	631
24 Others		454	...	...	685	818	587	558	21344	528	18028	18428
Total Amer.		1507	14	1043	6330	6108	3753	4897	160564	5972	250931	221452
Percentage American		‡ 34	27	20	36	30	37	41	35	66	62	51
LMS	1798	154	4	177	733	1159	795	885	34398	469	18863	12922
CMS	1813	494	11	569	4118	3933	217	1673	79196		† 15697	31256
WMS	1815	203	6	244	446	2504	782	1031	59143	871	36047	14136
SPG	1820	203	7	709	1076	1690	808	793	35738		† 15956	38406
UFC	1823	175	4	1757	454	749	130	286	15068	200	10275	3391
CSM	1830	96	3	778	168	363	126	198	8776		† 772	2303

25 Others	812	0	0	1875	1724	952	976	37247	759	38785	22598
Total Brit.	2137	35	4234	8870	12122	3810	5842	269566	2299	136395	125012
Percentage British ‡	48	67	79	50	60	38	49	56	25	34	29
9 Continental	481	0	0	985	1174	569	558	36387	489	12487	85128
17 International or Indian	274	3	63	1238	516	1888	516	11271	228	1209	1075
Grand Total	4399	52	5340	17423	19920	10020	11813	477788	8988	401022	432667

* Number of teachers not given in the Report, so one teacher is credited to each school. There are, of course, more. † Catechumens. ‡ These rows give the percentages of the American and British Societies' totals respectively to the whole number in each column.

THE GROWTH OF MISSIONARY EDUCATION BY DECADES.

	1830	1851	1861	1871	1881	1891	1901	1905
Female Pupils	2000	16441	25284	32147	72648	123575	169686 *	
Male Pupils	28000	63855	74875	111372	168998	218145	291177	
Total Pupils	30000	80296	100159	143519	241646	341720	460863	527660†
Sunday School Pupils		?	?	?	83321	160820	319651	401022
Communicant Members		17306	47274	78494	145097	223941	355720	432667
Nominal Christians ‡		102951	213373	318363	528590	671285	1012463	?
Population of India		¶	¶	240931521	256396646	289187316	294361056	

* In this figure are included 39949 Zenana Pupils.
† In this figure are included 9923 Industrial School Pupils, and also Zenana Pupils as before.
‡ Protestants. ¶ The first census for all India was taken in 1872.

BIBLIOGRAPHY.

I. GOVERNMENT AND OTHER OFFICIAL PUBLICATIONS.

Halifax Despatch of 1854.

Report of the Education Commission, 1882.

Report of the Indian Universities Commission, 1902.

Resolution of the Government of India on Indian Educational Policy, 1904.

The Educational Policy of the State of India, being a Reprint of Portions of all the Above. Satakopachari and Co., Madras.

Indian Census Reports for 1901.

Quinquennial Report of Education in India, 1897-1902, London. (The same for 1902-1907 has appeared since writing this Thesis.)

Report of the Director of Public Instruction, Madras: Annual.

Madras Educational Rules, 1906.

Madras Grant-in-aid Code, 1906.

General Report on Public Instruction in Bengal: Annual.

Report on Public Instruction in the Punjab: Annual.

Report on Public Instruction in Bombay: Annual.

Report on Public Instruction in Burma: Annual.

Calendars of the Following Universites: (Annual) Calcutta; Bombay; Madras; Allahabad; Punjab.

II. MISSIONARY CONFERENCE REPORTS. (Interdenominational).

Conferences meeting in England: Liverpool, 1860.

Mildmay, London, 1878. London, 1888.

Conferences meeting in America: Chicago, Congress of Missions, 1893. New York, Ecumenical, 1900.

Conferences meeting in India: Calcutta (Provincial), 1855.

Ootacamund (South India), 1858. Punjab, 1862-63.

Allahabad, (All India Decennial), 1872-73. Bangalore (South India) 1879. Calcutta (All India Decennial), 1882-83.

Bombay (All India Decennial), 1892-93.

Madras (South India), 1900. Madras (All India Decennial), 1902.

III. ANNUAL REPORTS OF MISSIONARY SOCIETIES WORKING IN INDIA. (Those of the last ten years have been specially consulted.)

Statistical Tables of Protestant Missions in India, Baptist Mission Press, Calcutta 1872; 1882; 1892; 1902.

Husband, Rev. John, Protestant Missionary Directory; Ajmer, 1906.

Special Report of the Committee for the Propagation of the Gospel in Foreign Parts to the General Assembly of the Church of Scotland, on Educational Missions in India; Edinburgh, 1890.

IV. BIOGRAPHIES AND HISTORIES.

Smith, Dr. George: Life of William Carey; London, 1887.

Smith, Dr. George: Life of John Wilson; London, 1879.

Smith, Dr. George: Life of Alexander Duff; London, 1881. (Also reprinted in New York.)

Morris, Henry: Life of John Murdoch; London, 1906.

Holcomb, Helen H: Lives of Robert Noble and John Anderson, in Men of Might in India Missions; New York.

Creegan, Rev. C. C.: Life of William Miller, in Pioneer Missionaries of the Church; New York, 1903.

Duff, Dr. Alexander: India and India Missions.

Sherring, Rev. M. A.: History of Protestant Missions in India; London, 1884.

Anderson, Rev. Rufus: Missions of the American Board in India; Boston, 1874.

Stock; Eugene: History of the Church Missionary Society; London, 1899

Lovett, Richard: History of the London Missionary Society; London, 1899.

Gordon, A: Our India Missions. (United Presbyterian Church).

Hunter, R: History of Missions of the Free Church of Scotland in India; London.

Smith, Dr. George: The Conversion of India; New York, 1893.

V. General Works bearing on Missionary Education in India.

Trevelyan, Sir Charles: Education of the People of India; 1838.

Thomas, F. W.: British Education in India; Cambridge, 1891.

Chamberlain, Dr. William I.: Education in India; New York, 1899.

Warneck, Dr. Gustav: Missions Lehre, Volume III, Part 2, pp. 130-171. Gotha.

Dennis, Dr. James S.: Christian Missions and Social Progress, Volume I, pp. 357-361. Volume II, pp. 35 ff. Volume III, pp. 1-127; 1899-1906.

Mott, John R.: Strategic Points in the World's Conquest.

Wilder, Rev. R. G.: Mission Schools in India; New York, 1861.

Wilder, Robert P: Among India's Students; New York, 1899.

Murdoch, Dr. John: Indian Missionary Manual; London, 1895.

Thoburn, Bishop James M.: The Christian Conquest of India; Boston, 1906.

Curzon in India: Reports of Speeches, etc. New York, 1906.

BIOGRAPHICAL NOTE.

Henry Huizinga was born near Zeeland, Michigan, Jan. 8th, 1873. He was graduated from Hope College, Holland, Mich., in 1893, and he spent the next three years as a student of theology in the Theological Seminary of the Reformed Church in America at the same place. At the same time he qualified for the degree of Master of Arts at Hope College. From 1896 to 1906 he was engaged in missionary educational work in India and also pursued the study of both the Tamil and Telugu languages. In September, 1906 he joined the Graduate School of the University of Michigan and pursued the study of the Science and Art of Teaching under Professor Whitney during two semesters and the summer session of 1907, and continued under the direction of this department after the close of the summer school till November. He also took up courses in Sanskrit Literature under Professor Meader and in English Literature under Professor Demmon. He left for India on the 5th November, to resume his work in the college at Ongole.

INDEX.

The figures refer to the pages.

Abbreviations, 129.
Aim of Missionary Education, 95-104.
—Among non-Christians, 98-104.
American Societies, 16, 51-53, 75-77, 134.
Anderson, Rev. John, 47-49, 81.
Area of India, 1.
Auckland, Lord, 34, 35.
Bangalore Conference, 113.
Baptists, American, 51, 52, 75, 76, 134.
Baptist Missionary Society (English), 10-12, 53, 134.
Bentinck, Lord, a helper to Duff, 22.
—Bentinck's Proclamation of 1835, 30; Opinion of Duff, 31.
Bibliography, 136-138.
Canadian Presbyterian Mission, 76, 134.
Carey, Wm, 10-12.
Cathedral Mission College, 55.
Christian Community and Education, 90, 91, 95, 96.
Christian Literature Society, 49, 50.
Christian Readers, 122, 123.
Christian Teachers, 117-119.
Christian Vernacular Education Society, 49, 50.
Church Missionary Society, 14-16, 54-56, 77, 78.
Colleges, 75-82, 97, 130-133.
Commission of 1882, The Education, 58-71.
Commission of 1902, Universities, 82-88.
—Curzon, Lord, 83, 84.
Congregationalists, American, 16, 51, 75, 134.
Cooke, Miss, Work in Calcutta, 17.
Dennis, Rev. J. S., 114, 115.
Duff, Alexander, 19-36, 43, 80.
Dufferin, Lord, 113.
Dutch Reformed Church in Ceylon, 8, 9.
Education Ancient, 2.
Education Commission of 1882, The, 58-71.
Ewing, Rev. J. C. R., 74.
Examinations in the Bible, 106, 107.
Expenditure on Missionary Education, 91-93.
Female Education, 56, 57, 69, 70, 90, 91.
Friendliness of mission school pupils to mission work, 107-109.
Girls' Education, see Female Education.
Government Education, 6, 59-61, 84.
Government, Relation of Missionary Education to, 6, 7, 58-61, 65-71, 85-88.
Grant-in-aid, First, 13.
Grants-in-aid, 59, 60, 66, 67.
Halifax Despatch, 36-42.
Harding's Minute, Lord, 35.

High schools, 63, 96, 97.
Hunter, Sir Wilson W., 61.
Independent Societies, 16, 17, 132
Indigenous Education, 6, 62.
Invasions, Political & Spiritual, 3.
Jay Narayan's College, 15, 55.
Jesuit, early attempts, 8.
Kaiser-i-Hind, gold medals, 74.
London Missionary Society, 12-14, 54, 79.
Lutherans, American, 76, 77, 134.
Mackichan, Rev. D., 74, 80.
Madras Christian College, 47-49, 73, 74, 81.
Madras Decennial Conference, 114, 120, 121.
Methodists, American, 52, 77, 134.
Methods of mission work, 4, 89.
Middleton's College, Bishop, 14.
Miller, Dr. William, 61, 73-74, 101-103.
Missionaries engaged in Educational work, Number of, 91, 119-121.
Moral Education, 64.
Moral influence of Christian Education, 111.
Mott, John, R., 116.
Muhammadan Invasions, 3.
Muhammadans, Education among, 90, 91.
Muir, Sir William, 55, 113.
Murdoch, Dr. John, 49, 50, 122-123.
Nagercoil, 13.
Needs of Missionary Education, 116-128.
Noble College, 55.
Population and Education, 59, 70, 83, 89-91, 126-128.
Presbyterians, American, 52, 76, 134.
Primary Education, 59, 62.
Problems of Missionary Education, 117-128.
Rammohun Roy, 23, 24.
Reformed Church in America, 51, 76, 134.
Relation of Missionary Education to Government, 6, 7, 58-61, 65-71, 85-88.
Relation of Missionary Education to environment, 123-125.
Religious Education, 25, 65, 121-123, 125.
Results of Missionary Education, 105-116.
Scottish Missionary Society, 14, 53, 80.
Scotland, United Free Church of, (see also Duff, Wilson, Anderson, Miller, Mackichan), 79-82, 134.
Second Grade Colleges, 85, 86.
Serampore College, 11, 12, 14, 54.
Social Progress, 110, 112.
Society for the Propagation of the Gospel, 14, 78, 79, 134.
St. John's College, 55-56.
Statistics, 18, 56, 57, 70, 88-94, 129-135.
Statistics not the only results, 105.
Swartz, 10.
Testimony to the value of Missionary Education, 31, 112-116.
Training of Christian workers, 9, 49, 50, 96.
Tranquebar, Early work in, 9.
Trevelyan, Sir Charles, 28, 29.
United Presbyterians, 76, 134.
United Free Church of Scotland, see Scotland.
Unity of Aim in Educational work, 103, 104.
Universities Commission of 1902, 82-88.
Warneck, Dr. Gustav, 114, 115.
Wesleyan Missionary Society, 79, 134.
Wilson, Rev. John, 43-47, 80.
Wilson College, 43-47, 80.
Xavier's College at Goa, 8.